IN THEIR OWN HANDS

Can young people change Australia?

Lucas Walsh and Rosalyn Black

with

James Arvanitakis and Eric Sidoti

Johanna Wyn

Thom Woodroofe

ACER Press

First published 2011
by ACER Press, an imprint of
Australian Council *for* Educational Research Ltd
19 Prospect Hill Road, Camberwell
Victoria, 3124, Australia

www.acerpress.com.au
sales@acer.edu.au

The Foundation for Young Australians has supported
the publication of *In Their Own Hands*. The programs
conducted by The Foundation for Young Australians are
subject to change. The programs described in this book are
current at time of writing.

Edited by Maureen O'Keefe
Cover design, text design and typesetting by ACER Project Publishing
Indexed by Russell Brooks
Printed in Australia by BPA Print Group

National Library of Australia Cataloguing-in-Publication entry:

Author:	Walsh, Lucas, 1969-
Title:	In their own hands : can young people change Australia? / Lucas Walsh and Rosalyn Black.
ISBN:	9781742860114 (pbk.)
Notes:	Includes index.
Subjects:	Youth—Political activity—Australia. Social change—Australia. Youth—Leadership.
Other Authors/Contributors:	Black, Rosalyn, 1959-
Dewey Number:	305.242

Foreword

Cheryl Kernot

Once in a rare while, the fundamental architecture of a significant part of society shifts. Over the last two and one-half decades, the organization of the social half of society, led by social entrepreneurs, has done so.

Ashoka founder, Bill Drayton, 2002

In their actions and aspirations the profound value changes led by young Australians are evident and compelling: they are looking for new institutions to stand up and make a change; they are less forgiving of purely for-profit driven corporations; and they are looking for ways in which they can personally contribute to change. A 21st century call to action!

The last 30 years has witnessed a complex and accelerating interrelationship between globalisation, an internet and communications revolution, a 700 per cent increase in per capita wealth in developed market economies, the spread of democracy, and increased literacy and education.

Access to information coupled with growing demands for transparency and accountability has contributed to a collapse of faith in hierarchies such as traditional politics and the church, exposed the negative social impacts of deregulated free markets and the failure of centralised public sector solutions, and shown many traditional institutions as unable to respond to the unmet social challenges of our time.

Television and the internet mean we can no longer be far away from the visible poverty and suffering of our fellow humans and the impacts of the escalating environmental, health and economic crises: of global warming, mass extinctions of species, depleted resources rendering three billion 'water stressed'; the AIDS pandemic predicted to affect 100 million globally by 2010; and economic inequality whereby the poorest 50 per cent account for 5 per cent of global income.

We cannot remain ignorant of the recent global financial crisis and the way it demonstrates one aspect of the retreat of government in the face of free market ideology: the rise of corporate power. In 2008, 300 multinational corporations accounted for 25 per cent of global assets, some with greater wealth than nations.

This is the world our young adults have inherited.

But the good news is that the growth of the middle class in many countries, along with increased access to higher education, has added to the ranks of people who possess both the knowledge and the financial means to tackle social problems effectively. Young social entrepreneurs are part of this.

Social entrepreneurs are society's drivers of change. Together with institutions, networks and communities, social entrepreneurs create solutions that are efficient, sustainable, transparent and have measurable impact. They apply traditional business tools to create profit for reinvestment in the core social purpose of their businesses, not to maximise the wealth of individual shareholders.

The Skoll Centre for Social Entrepreneurship at Oxford University where I worked for several years says 'ultimately, social entrepreneurship is aimed at transformational systems change that tackles the root causes of poverty, marginalisation, environmental deterioration and the accompanying loss of human dignity. The key concepts of social entrepreneurship are innovation, market orientation and systems change.' Key concepts for which young people have both a skill set and a driving passion.

Social entrepreneurs don't accept the notion that only governments and corporations are best positioned to determine how resources should be allocated. In the coming decade, individuals have the potential to make positive changes on a global scale, bypassing the institutions of last century which are either too bureaucratic or too inflexible to respond in an innovative way.

Muhammad Yunus' Grameen Bank changed the world's financial systems with his pioneering of microfinance. Jessica and Matt Flannery were in their early twenties when they built on this innovation, devising Kiva, an online lending platform that allows individuals in the developed world to lend small amounts of money to small business people in the developing world: a spinach farmer in Cambodia, a beekeeper in Ghana, a fish-seller in Uganda were among their first. As young people they appreciated the power of social media and used Web 2.0 to drive social change. They also understood the power of a loan compared with a charitable donation: the longer-term benefits of equity and economic self-sufficiency instead of dependency. Also, typically for their generation, they believe passionately in the power of human connection. Since starting in 2005 they have attracted US$60 million and now work in 40 countries (www.kiva.org).

It's not useful to be unrealistically romantic about the number of Young Social Pioneers in Australia but, given a more mature social finance system and an enabling government, the opportunities will be equally exciting as elsewhere in the world.

One of my current students runs Food Connect Sydney, a social business which supplies local, sustainably produced food from farmers living within a five-hour drive from Sydney, to the wider community in Sydney. Food Connect aims to create a new, more equitable way of distributing local produce in a socially responsible way. Its emphasis is on seasonal produce which comes from local farmers who are paid a fair price for their hard work and who are encouraged to farm using the most sustainable methods possible. Boxes of freshly picked fruit and vegetables are collected by purchasers, from the homes of a network of 'city cousins.'

A second student runs 'Soft Landing', a pioneering social business which recycles mattresses and eliminates landfill. It trains and employs marginalised people, such as ex-offenders and local long-term unemployed people. It has a very sound business model ripe for expansion and the reinvestment of profits in its core social purposes.

As consumers, young Australians add social impact by giving voice to ethical consumption choices: the challenging of wage injustice by demanding fair trade coffee or by boycotting products made in sweatshops.

In workplaces, young Australians have a big impact on the corporate social responsibility agenda of the companies they choose to work for. It is commonplace for young interviewees to ask about the corporate citizenship policies of prospective employers and the role of their company in effecting positive social change.

If you like to embrace change as I do it's a great time to be a young adult, with the global landscape offering new forms of partnerships, new ways of doing business, new ways of networking and new forms of social finance. I have lived to see some Treasuries now talking about the measurement of social value creation alongside the previously one-dimensional financial approach; this is recognition of the interconnectedness of all we do. That's been my call to action for most of my life.

Cheryl Kernot is Director of Social Business
at the Centre for Social Impact.

Contents

Introduction

A dual view of young people and change

This book draws on our experience, as well as the experience of our colleagues and contributors, to provide a critical overview of the conditions, emerging trends and approaches that influence the capacity and disposition of young people to engage and actively participate in shaping their world. Providing this overview has presented some genuine challenges to us as authors, challenges that point toward the fundamentally bifocal view that persists in relation to young people, social action and change.

Working at The Foundation for Young Australians (FYA), we have ample and frequent exposure to politically and civically active young people who are engaged, innovative and hopeful. We are in the highly privileged position of working with young people who are participating creatively in their schools, driving action within their communities and leading brave and bold initiatives for widespread social change. We see and document the impact and outcomes of their actions, both for themselves as individuals and for the contexts in which they are seeking to make a difference. We also observe the growth and spread of initiatives that promise to expand young people's spheres of influence and to encourage greater numbers of young people to exert this influence. At the same time, we are constantly building and contributing to a body of research evidence that suggests another view: a view of young people who are disengaged, discouraged, apathetic and excluded.

As a result, our analysis also has a dual perspective.

On the one hand, it is predicated on our strong belief that young people's participation in society is a highly desirable good in and of itself.

This is a central tenet of FYA as an organisation. It is reflected in our own initiatives and in the initiatives we support, some of which are described in the case studies that make up an important part of this book. It underpins the research we conduct and the research we support, some of which is described in our commentaries. It is also predicated on our conviction that young people's participation has numerous positive outcomes for the wider social good.

On the other hand, our analysis is informed by the evident challenges that confront the genuine and meaningful participation of young people in domains such as schooling, political participation, local government and everyday life. These challenges are pervasive. They emerge from the research. They emerge from the observations of key experts across all of these domains. Most tellingly, they emerge from the accounts of young people seeking to make a difference.

In her Foreword, Cheryl Kernot discusses the exciting possibilities for change in contemporary Australia. This book explores these possibilities within the context of the complex challenges faced by young people in making change. What emerges from this book, then, is a picture of young people's participation that is characterised by deep structural constraints and disengagement on the one hand and by strong policy directions and innovation on the other. From the authors' perspective, this means that complacency is impossible. Some of the developments described in this book are genuinely exciting, encouraging and inspiring. They lend themselves readily to an uncritical or breathless valorisation of young people's role in society and their potential to reshape a range of important social, economic and political outcomes for Australia. Other trends and developments are more worrying. Their depiction and consideration could easily plunge us into gloom.

Instead, our stance as authors is to celebrate the successes and encouraging signals for young people's participation and citizenship while critically examining the barriers to its growth and effectiveness. We hope that this book will endorse, authorise and inspire existing and new efforts to give young people the respect, recognition and space that they deserve across the full range of civic and political structures. We also hope that it will help to avoid the uncritical adoption of tokenistic mechanisms that pay lip service to the notion of active citizenship but do little to advance it. Too many youth forums, for example, which claim to engage young people fail to do any more than canvass views and be self-serving. Our intention is to provide a set of useful signals about the potential for core social institutions and processes to rethink the way in which they engage with young people. And we hope that it will serve as a platform for further thinking and for action.

About the structure of this book

This book is made up of three chapters, each of which explores one or more domains for young people's participation and leadership. Each chapter opens with a viewpoint provided by expert thinkers, practitioners and observers which provide a thumbnail sketch of key issues and trends within the domain. Each chapter then provides a case study or collection of case studies that illustrate how young people are participating, or attempting to participate within it. Finally, each chapter concludes with a critical review by the authors of the literature, the empirical evidence and the theoretical arguments for young people's participation in shaping their futures. This combination of expert opinion, case studies of practice and analysis is intended to enrich our collective understanding of young people's participation.

Chapter 1 describes young people's inclusion, political participation and experience of active citizenship.

The first viewpoint is provided by James Arvanitakis and Eric Sidoti, who reflect on their research. They begin their reflections in 2008 at a meeting organised under the auspices of the Whitlam Institute, where around 50 change-makers took part in a conversation as part of a larger project working with young people to imagine a new democracy. The majority of these change-makers were under 25 years old. Many came from youth peak bodies or organisations such as the Australian Youth Climate Coalition and Get Up! Seeking to understand the changing nature of political engagement amongst young people, Eric and James find that young people are participating in informal political settings and in relation to specific issues, while eschewing conventional mainstream or big 'P' politics. They find that many young people are politically ambivalent. Many have an entrenched distrust of formal politics. Many disengage from politics entirely. This broader disengagement is evident in poor levels of voter registration amongst 18 to 25 year olds. It suggests that too many young Australians lack confidence, knowledge and opportunity. A pivotal message here is the importance of civic and political participation in developing, challenging and affirming the agency of young people.

The first case study puts this message in perspective through its account of the experiences of three young people seeking to make change in their communities. Their experiences echo those described by Cheryl Kernot in the Foreword. They express a desire to bypass slow bureaucracy, but appreciate the importance of partnership and networks. Their independence enables them to deliver initiatives more quickly, directly and effectively than their counterparts in local government, as well as to tackle issues too sensitive for established institutions. Each of these young people is seeking to address the needs of people experiencing exclusion, ranging from advocating for same-sex attracted young people in rural Victoria (OUTthere), to connecting remote Indigenous and non-Indigenous youth in remote regions (Linkz). Each is a participant in Young Social Pioneers (YSP), a program conducted by FYA based on the International Youth Foundation's Youth Action Net, which seeks to empower socially conscious young people who create positive change in their communities to become successful leaders.

Lucas Walsh closes Chapter 1 by investigating the extent to which active citizenship, as proposed in the *Melbourne Declaration on Educational Goals for Young Australians*, is possible given the different ways that young people feel marginalised, alienated and excluded (MCEETYA, 2008). His commentary investigates the nature of citizenship and its relevance to the needs and experiences of young people in Australia. Lucas proposes that the quality and extent of any given person's participation in the development and decision-making processes of a community will depend on the nature and quality of that person's membership within it. He argues that exclusion and marginalisation from political, cultural and economic domains of young people's lives delimits the possibility for experiencing full membership as a basis for active citizenship. Young people's experiences of marginalisation from political decision-making and economic participation, as well as exclusion through racism and prejudice, demand a more sophisticated and rigorous conceptualisation and realisation of citizenship that is more than a legal status and which is relevant to the real lives of young people.

Chapter 2 looks at young people's participation in and through their schools.

In the second viewpoint, Johanna Wyn provides key insights and examples of how student participation can be used to address entrenched patterns of educational disadvantage. Johanna's perspective understands schools as political and cultural organisations that can be conducive to negative patterns of inequality as much as positive transformation. Curriculum, for example, is a cultural tool that can reinforce inequalities between students. Johanna argues that, despite good evidence, young people are still not taken seriously and continue to be excluded from participating in decisions about their education. She also provides positive examples of participation that place a high value on the capacity of students to make valuable contribution to learning in their school.

These examples are amplified by the case study of the ruMAD? (are you Making A Difference?) program. This has been operating in Australian primary and secondary schools for a decade, originally through Education Foundation and now through FYA, providing a framework for young people to leverage change within their schools, their immediate local community and, in some cases, more far-flung locations and settings. The story from Melbourne Girls' College demonstrates both what young people can do and how schools can foster a climate of participation that permeates classroom practice and redefines learning.

As a counter to these stories, Rosalyn Black's commentary points out that while schools are regularly identified as key sites for young people's participation, this rhetoric is not always reflected in what takes place at the chalkface. Her commentary examines some of the tensions between the mandate for young people's social participation that is provided by current educational policy in Australia and the way in which Australian schools and schooling support this participation in practice. It also examines how emerging state and federal policy directions affect the capacity of schools to support young people's participation.

Despite the occasionally bleak views of participation by young people within the political, social and educational institutions described in Chapters 1 and 2, other vehicles for social and political communication and participation, such as new media and social enterprise, open up new opportunities. These are described in Chapter 3.

The final viewpoint comes from 2009 Young Victorian of the Year, Thom Woodroofe, who provides an autobiographical perspective of his journey from a country town to establish Left Right Think-Tank, an independent and non-partisan think-tank for young people. In the Foreword, Cheryl Kernot suggests that young people are wary of government bureaucracy and corporations driven purely by profit motives. This wariness is evident in Thom's observations of young people who are 'sick of partisan politics and eager to focus on the substance of ideas'. Contrary to the concerns of some over what are perceived to be declining levels of youth engagement and participation, Thom's experience and research suggests that young people are involved, but that the paradigm of involvement has shifted to more entrepreneurial and democratic forms of participation.

The case study of SYN provides a positive example of how information and communication technologies (ICTs) can enhance and expand young people's communication and engagement.

This paves the way for the concluding commentary by Lucas Walsh, which explores the emergence of social enterprises in recent years and how they are using technology to enhance their day-to-day operations, networks and impact. The usage of ICTs has shifted as a result of developments such as Web 2.0 tools, platforms and approaches. With this shift, social enterprises have been able to extend their influence and networks, as well as challenge conventional loci of power. Some ongoing challenges are identified, including barriers of access and digital literacy. The nature of online participation is also interrogated. It is suggested that understanding the real value of ICTs is difficult given the hyperbole and lack of tangible evidence of sustained social impact. Nevertheless, the nimble, adaptable and innovative ways that social enterprises can use ICTs to meet the challenges of the 21st century suggests exciting new opportunities for young people to engage in social action and change-making.

Acknowledgements

The authors are very grateful to all contributors for their thought-provoking insights, with particular thanks to case study participants for giving us their scarce time and sharing their experiences. We acknowledge the inspiration and support provided by our colleagues at FYA. The authors would like to acknowledge the research contribution of Dr Barbara Lemon (formerly Coordinator of Research and Evaluation with FYA) to the case studies. Particular thanks go to Celia Hannon for her invaluable input in the development of our thinking. Enormous thanks also to Emma Rujevic for her editorial feedback.

References

Ministerial Council on Education, Employment, Training and Youth Affairs (MCEETYA). (2008). *Melbourne Declaration on Educational Goals for Young Australians*. Retrieved 31 March 2011 from: http://www.mceecdya.edu.au/mceecdya/melbourne_declaration,25979.html

Note about terminology

The publisher and authors are aware that the preferred terminology is Aboriginal and Torres Strait Islander peoples when referring to First Australians. In this title, however, the term Indigenous is used because this is the terminology in the original source documents being discussed.

In or out?

CHAPTER 1

Viewpoint 1:

The politics of change – where to for young people and politics

James Arvanitakis and Eric Sidoti

On a sunny Saturday in September 2008, the Whitlam Institute and its partners at the University of Western Sydney invited some 50 'change-makers' to the State Library of New South Wales to take part in a democratic conversation. Appropriately, the State Library adjoins the Parliament of New South Wales in Macquarie Street very near Government House and the origins of government in Australia.

Counted among those present were some 20 or so experienced (read 'older') change-makers from the unions, politics, business, education, consumer and other social movements. A slightly greater number were under 25 years old. This was a diverse group; some came from a base in organisations such as the Australian Youth Climate Coalition, Get Up! or youth peak bodies; other individuals had carved a reputation in science or publishing or information technology.

There was little structure and no pre-determined agenda to the day. Conversation, though, was animated and robust from start to finish. What became clear as the day progressed was that all present, regardless of age or background, shared a conviction that we can shape our society notwithstanding the complexities and limitations that may exist. What emerged just as clearly was the sense that this conviction was bred of experience: everyone present had been motivated to action on something that mattered to them and in doing so had, to employ that over-used phrase, 'made a difference' in some way. The younger Australians present were generally confident and engaged and could be said to be politically savvy within their own spheres of activity.

Our democratic conversation was one part of a larger project on working with young people to imagine a new democracy. In the process, we were attempting to understand the changing nature of political engagement and whether young people were as disengaged as the popular media would have us believe. It threw into stark relief what the more formal research had been revealing.

Young people are politically engaged while Politically ambivalent

Contrary to the popular belief that young people are apathetic, the research suggests that young people are active in the broader 'everyday' politics of their communities and in the support of the particular causes or issues that matter to them (Collin, 2008). The extent of this engagement within 'informal politics' – or small 'p' politics – is disguised to some extent because it adopts forms that are often not understood, and frequently dismissed. As one participant in our research put it: 'Young people are already active – just in ways not always understood' (Arvanitakis & Marren, 2009, p. 6).

At the same time, there is an apparently entrenched distrust of and distance from formal Politics (or big 'P' politics) among large numbers of young people. The Australian Government's *Electoral Reform Green Paper* (2009), for example, notes that only 82 per cent of eligible 18 to 25 year olds were enrolled to vote as of 30 June 2008. Though this represents an increase of 1.0 per cent from the previous year, reflecting a determined effort by the Australian Electoral Commission to increase registration, the fact remains that over an extended period roughly one in five young people have not enrolled to vote. Voter registration might be seen as a proxy for the health or otherwise of the relationship between young people as citizens and the State. Such a figure, we believe, should therefore be a warning sign and not dismissed as something that will sort itself out.

Our research clearly found that young people, for diverse reasons, are participating in activities that deliver short-term, visible and efficacious outcomes that eschew traditional hierarchies, operate through transparent processes and afford agency. They neither believe that they have all the answers nor do they seek unrealistic responsibility, but they do want to be involved in decision-making processes. However, they express frustration that their participation in formal Political institutions and processes are neither acknowledged nor seen as relevant.

If we are genuinely interested in encouraging young people's engagement in democratic politics then it is important that we understand the activities they do pursue, what motivates it, what forms it takes and what impact it is having. It is important that we nurture rather than suppress their enthusiasm and commitment.

The success with which we can bridge this chasm between broad civic engagement and a more active engagement in the politics of public policy and government will determine the nature and health of Australian democracy in the 21st century. While the focus here is on younger Australians, there is sufficient evidence to suggest that these are more fundamental trends across the broader population (Arvanitakis & Marren, 2009).

The idea of citizenship

In his monumental work, *The Life and Death of Democracy*, John Keane argues that the history of democracy can be understood in three broad phases (Keane, 2009a). Its origins can be characterised as assembly-based democracy. This was followed by the period of representative democracy with which we are familiar. Our supposed familiarity, though, may be misplaced as Keane suggests that in the post-1945 period we have entered what he calls monitory democracy. In this democratic era, power is subject to the scrutiny of multiple institutions – not just the parliament and the courts but human rights bodies and frameworks, professional organisations and civic initiatives – in a time of 'communicative abundance' in which global communication has become a reality (Keane, 2009b). In the age of monitory democracy, he argues, 'cross-border and global power relations are now equally important shapers of citizens' lives' (Keane, 2009c, p. 72).

Whether or not you support Keane's conclusions – and we, at least, have some reservations – his depiction of the age resonates very strongly with our own findings with respect to young people's engagement. Both give rise to a need for renewed discussions about citizenship in the modern era.

In this respect we would suggest a start might be made by looking at three focal points. The first is the need to consider the fluid, heterogeneous nature of citizenship in a rapidly changing and complex world. The second is to complement the common 'top-down' approach, focusing on what is expected of citizens, with greater consideration of what citizens desire given their emergent ways of understanding the world. The third is the need to recognise that citizenship today may involve connections across the world, as well as more immediate, local forms of action. Family and kinship networks, dual citizenship, labour mobility and multiple lived experiences mean that we need to understand that citizenship is more complex than could have been imagined even a generation ago.

In short, citizens are no longer stable, homogenised, nor bound to a single nation and place: younger Australians live this new reality.

With the assistance of Professor Bob Hodge from the University of Western Sydney's Centre for Cultural Research, we have developed the following typology in an attempt to give some order to this complexity as we grapple with notions of engagement and empowerment as key determinants of what others might refer to as active citizenship. The typology seeks to take account of recent research suggesting that defining 'citizenship' in rigid, restrictive terms, privileging a limited range of values and identities, and then imposing this concept on young people exacerbates a sense of exclusion and alienation (Arvanitakis & Marren, 2009). It posits citizenship, for example, as something that young people are expected to 'grow into': a process that both ignores changing markers of adulthood as well as the many contributions that young people are making to our society (Collin, 2008).

In Figure 1 we identify four forms of citizenship, only one of which describes what might generally be understood as the 'optimal' or 'ideal' citizen who is both fully engaged and empowered. The arrows indicate the dynamic nature of this strategic map. Each of these types potentially includes diverse possibilities, as any individual citizen's place in this matrix will change according to circumstance and the dynamic processes of everyday life.

In Type A, Marginalisation and Citizenship Deficit, the citizenship deficit is driven by a belief among those in this group that interaction with civic institutions is pointless as their opinions and demands will be ignored. There is little or no connection with the civic institutions surrounding them. These people feel that any effort to be involved will have no results, so that a sense of disengagement and disempowerment prevails. This attitude may arise from either personal experience or the encounters others from the same family or background may have had with civic institutions. While not always the case, our research suggests that many young people fit into this group and, as you might expect, similarly those from lower socio-economic backgrounds.

Type A, however, does not preclude citizenship deficits applying to wealthy populations. A lack of interaction with civic institutions because of privatisation, or even neglect by government, may lead to the privatisation of decision-making and withdrawal from the public arena and democratic processes. Such citizens find their relationships with civic institutions more like that of consumers. Sometimes described as 'aspirationals', these people

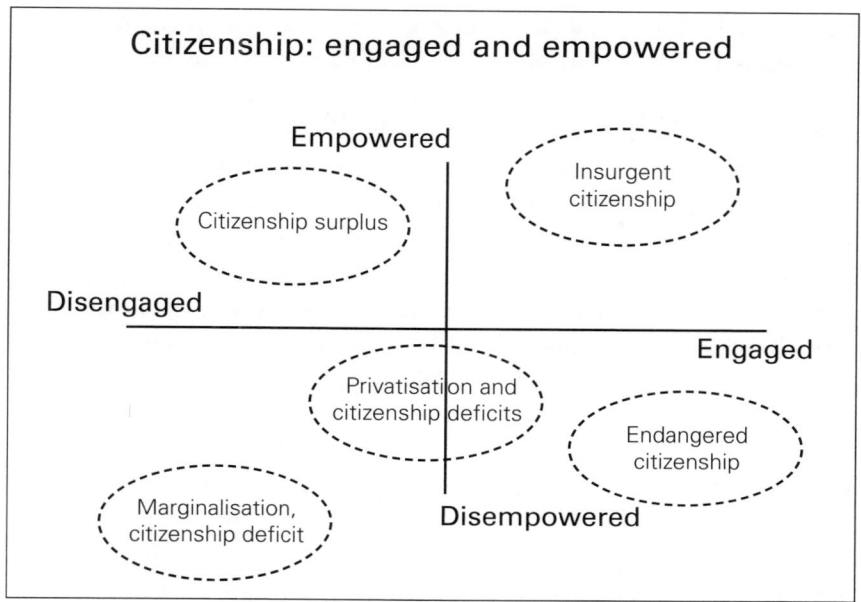

Figure 1: Typology of Citizenship Deficit and Surplus

may feel empowered during times of economic boom; during times of economic contraction this quickly dissipates.

Type C, Citizenship Surplus, groups those who are empowered but not engaged. These citizens are in 'surplus' notwithstanding their limited or negligible political engagement. While this group may appear to have much in common with those 'aspirationals' in Type A, their disengagement is a consequence of choice. Amongst this group there is a strong push for self-sufficiency – a belief that their social capital, wealth and status mean that they do not require the services of civic institutions (including government bodies). While not antagonistic towards such institutions, they believe that many services provided by the private sector are generally superior to public ones.

Type D, the Insurgent Citizen (see Holston, 2007), is both engaged and empowered. This group may not have access to many financial resources, but have high social capital and a willingness and ability to make time to be engaged in the political process. They feel empowered through their social background and determinedly engage with civic institutions and political processes. These citizens are ideologically defined: they may have progressive or conservative agendas.

Type B, Endangered Citizenship, is the zone of frustration and potentially one that poses the most immediate challenge to Australia's long-term democratic health. Those inhabiting this zone are engaged in political processes but find their way to genuine empowerment blocked for various reasons (including, for example, institutional racism). Finding the way barred despite their desire and effort to be engaged breeds frustration and anger that may lead to resignation (and an identification with Type A) or to conflict.

The critical implication of this analysis is that an individual citizen's relationship to the democratic polity is fluid, dependent on a range of factors including, but not restricted to, background and circumstance.

It is not unreasonable to suggest that these dynamics are all the more pronounced for young people, if only by virtue of the fact that youth is itself a period of change and discovery, of heightened emotions and experience.

Young citizens should be inspired not just wired

It is no exaggeration to suggest that we are entering a period during which Australian democracy will be up for grabs. For the moment, change is being left to the vagaries of circumstance. It is being driven by elemental forces.

Prominent among these is the 'new galaxy of media' defined, according to Keane, by the spirit of communicative abundance. New media and technologies dominate much of the research on political participation by young people and indeed much of the commentary on political trends; particularly in the wake of the unprecedented success of the Obama campaign.

These developments are fuelling the common conviction that new media and technologies are in themselves empowering young people and changing the very nature of politics, that they foreshadow an end to representative democracy as we have come to know it. Yet this conviction remains largely untested and, for the moment at least, lacks evidence. Our own project failed to unearth any substantive research on the actual political influence young people exert through the use of such technologies.

That said, there can be little doubt that young people are embracing the emergent communication technologies at a pace and breadth that is unprecedented – a development that is not limited to the Australian experience. They are utilising the technologies in undefined ways, expanding their social networks across previously segregated borders, to share experiences and information, to create their own 'news and views', and on occasion to mobilise and organise. It may well be that the most significant political influence of these new technologies will be the ability for young people to develop their own thinking and cultural norms in vast numbers through ever-widening circles of communication, without reference to the political mainstream or its institutions.

Whether this is desirable or democratically beneficial is the great unknown. No doubt for some it is nerve-racking; for others is it laced with the excitement of uncharted waters.

At the very least, the contribution that young people can make to the civic and political life of the nation through their utilisation of information and communication technologies (ICTs) should be acknowledged. There is virtue in exploring and promoting initiatives that offer practical and innovative opportunities for young people to engage in formalised political structures; these could include mechanisms such as digital storytelling, online workshops, petitions and forums. Decision-makers, often perceived by young people as operating within an 'old guard' information and communication mentality, could benefit from the experience, knowledge and initiative of young people in ICT usage, and open up not only opportunities for young people themselves but also for a positive dialogue about new ways of participation and engagement.

There is already much talk and some activity in this area. The Australian Government's Government 2.0 Task Force is one attempt to come to grips with these developments. Then Finance Minister, Lindsay Tanner (2009), stated that technology needed to encourage the involvement of the community in solving the many challenges facing Australia, noting that government must adapt to account for changing trends.

While we acknowledge that technology has the potential to further entrench inequalities, the broader framework available in new technologies means that the principles for a more open and responsive government are present.

Mark Elliott, Darren Sharp and Matt Cooperrider (2009), for example, argue that ICT tools can encourage 'crowdsourcing': that is, a method for the distributed production of ideas leading to greater efficiencies in knowledge generation. These methods create more open boundaries between governments, policy-makers and citizens and recognise that knowledge is widely distributed throughout society. This process of collaboration can include all participants having add/edit/delete rights to the same pool of content. This provides criteria by which to judge the relevance and applicability of collaboration to a project and encourages cooperation.

Government 2.0 should then also concern itself with making government and citizen interaction more collaborative and interactive and making government services more focused on the needs of the citizen. As such, it needs to be underpinned by democratic principles: universal access, transparency, and fairness among them.

Developments under the Government 2.0 umbrella, or similar initiatives, should not be considered in isolation. This is a point made by Miriam Lyons, Executive Director at the Centre for Policy Development, who argues that online tools should not be seen as replacing face-to-face public meetings or hard-copy publications, but used to supplement these, taking advantage of unique opportunities for increasing public participation in decision-making that they offer (2009).

In our view the fundamental point remains that the significance of the new media and technologies should be understood and embraced but should not be overstated nor relied upon to resolve the drift of younger Australians away from democratic politics.

New citizens in a new democracy

The more fundamental challenge is to open the doors to young people, recognising the place at the table of Australian democracy that is theirs by right. It has been said that rights turn beggars into claimants (Frankovits & Sidoti, 1995) and with a sense of one's rights comes dignity and confidence.

All those who participated in our democratic conversation on that Spring day in 2008, the younger change-makers very much included, had this in common. They did not wait to be invited to speak or to take up their cause or to agitate for change. As far as they are concerned, it is the natural thing to do in a democracy.

Yet, as our simple typology attempts to capture, this is by no means true for all citizens.

Too many young Australians lack the confidence or the knowledge or have been denied the opportunity. Too many have their way blocked: sometimes by institutional barriers such as an inadequate or inappropriate education; for others by cultural barriers; for others again by deeply embedded structural inequity.

The most critical lesson we take away from our work to date is that the single most important factor for a young person's civic and political participation is a sense of their own agency: the experience of having been involved in decision-making processes that generally respect their views and that deliver results in which those views are reflected even if not adopted.

How hard can it be for us – as parents, educators, service providers, healers, government officials, union organisers, employers and political party administrators – to do just that?

References

Arvanitakis, J., & Marren, S. (2009). *Putting the politics back into Politics: Young people and democracy in Australia.* Discussion paper. Sydney: Whitlam Institute.

Australian Government. (2009). *Electoral Reform Green Paper: Strengthening Australia's democracy.* Canberra: Australian Government.

Collin, P. (2008). *Young people imagining a new democracy.* Literature review. Sydney: Whitlam Institute.

Elliott, M., Sharp, D., & Cooperrider, M. (2009). 'Collaborating with the crowd for better policy development', Centre for Policy Development, 27 August, 2009, Sydney, Australia. Retrieved March 2011 from http://cpd.org.au/2009/08/case-study-collaborating-with-the-crowd-for-better-policy-development/

Frankovits, A., & Sidoti, E. (1995). *The rights way to development: A human rights approach to development assistance.* Sydney: Human Rights Council of Australia.

Holston, J. (2007). *Insurgent citizenship: Disjunctions of democracy and modernity in Brazil.* Princeton, NJ: Princeton University Press.

Keane, J. (2009a). *The life and death of democracy.* London: Simon & Schuster.

Keane, J. (2009b). 'Media Decadence and Democracy'. Senate Occasional Lecture Series, 28 August 2009. Parliament House, Canberra.

Keane, J. (2009c). Letter in 'Correspondence', *The Monthly*, 50, October 2009.

Lyons, M. (2009). 'Ideas for the Gov2.0 Taskforce: open sourcing policy development?' Centre for Policy Development, 27th August, 2009, Sydney Australia. Retrieved March 2011 from: http://cpd.org.au/2009/08/cpd-ideas-for-the-gov2-0-taskforce-open-sourcing-policy-development/

Tanner, L. (2009). 'Upgrading Democracy', Centre for Policy Development, 27 August, 2009, Sydney, Australia. Retrieved March 2011 from: http://cpd.org.au/2009/08/foreword-lindsay-tanner/

Dr James Arvanitakis is an academic-activist based at the Centre for Cultural Research at the University of Western Sydney and works with a number of youth-focused organisations.

Eric Sidoti is Director of the Whitlam Institute within the University of Western Sydney.

Case study 1:

Young Social Pioneers

Taking inspiration from the International Youth Foundation, the Young Social Pioneers program was established by FYA in 2009 with the aim of supporting and celebrating young people who are creating positive change in their communities. It provides tailored training in financial management and leadership skills, mentoring, personal development, and access to broad business networks. Many of the young people involved have set up their organisations in an attempt to take action on a particular issue that they feel is not being addressed by government. Though most would not describe themselves as politically active, their actions are in fact highly political. Their interaction with government and attitude to formal politics is complex.

Kathryn Ettwell and Jack Hegarty: OUTthere

I've been trying to educate myself a little bit lately about what's happening globally and learn more about other youth groups in other countries and the issues that they're facing. Even though I think Australia has a really warped definition of equality, I'm still glad I live here because, reading some of the things I've been reading, young gay activists being killed and such like that, I consider myself very lucky to have these opportunities to stand up for my rights, and to do it in a safe, formalised way. It really makes a difference for other young people. My experiences growing up weren't traumatising but they certainly had a big impact on my life, so to change that for future generations is a great opportunity.

(Kat Ettwell)

Both Kat and Jack are members of the OUTthere Rural Victorian Youth Council for Sexual Diversity, a lobby and advocacy group for same sex attracted young people in rural Victoria that provides resources and information to schools, youth services, communities and government departments. OUTthere is an initiative of the broader WayOut project, a partnership between Cobaw Community Health Service and Gay and Lesbian Health Victoria, with support from the Department of Health Services. The OUTthere youth council is part-funded by the Myer Foundation and comprises 15 young people representing half a dozen local groups across the state.

Kat and Jack are involved in local government in two different regional Victorian towns, and their attitudes to local government and the political process vary greatly. Kat left school in Year 10 to care for her mother, and became involved with the local youth services through a counsellor. It was:

> ... one of the ways that I managed to stay connected with the outside world ... that was my only social outlet ... any projects that were going on at the local council youth services, for my own sanity, when a seat opened up on that I put my hand up for it.

She joined the Youth Advisory Council for her local area and held her position for four years. She has served on the WayOut project for nine years and the OUTthere council for two.

For Kat, interaction with local government has been generally positive. As part of the Youth Advisory Council she remembers:

> We were very actively involved in the community ... whether it was community events or show days or information days, there would be a youth component and the youth council made sure that there was a youth presence at community events. One of the first things that we ever did was we used to run local youth forums and invite 30-odd students, a busload of students, from each of the four or five high schools in the area. The very first one we ran was really successful and the report that came out of that was praised by the local council. They were very thankful that we'd brought those issues to their attention, because they hadn't had that input into any of their meetings before so it really brought youth issues onto their agenda.

Jack, on the other hand, has found his local council apathetic at best: 'Half the young people wouldn't know who our representatives are. I don't even know who the mayor is'. Also, unlike Kat, he has found little satisfaction through the usual channels for youth participation:

> *The council has young councillors, like a youth group thing. They just do not represent young people in the [area]. It's like the top 10 people in the top 10 percentile of people, you know ... they don't know about youth issues, they play World of Warcraft on the weekend, they don't go out and ... experience things. It's like the one person multiplied.*

As part of their respective OUTthere groups, Kat and Jack have taken part in submissions to government inquiries into violence, youth suicide, and human rights, but both express a sense of alienation from the political process. Jack in particular is disillusioned with the local council: 'They seem almost untouchable ... I think there's this trend that if you want to change something in local government, you can only do it from the outside'.

Where Jack and his local OUTthere group have met with more success is in their approach to local schools. The OUTthere youth council acknowledges that resource packs provided by government to discourage homophobia in schools have minimal impact, and as part of its education campaign it advocates for the extension of safe sex education programs to cover same sex attracted young people. The appointment of a new principal and a collection of new and pre-service teachers at the local high school has created an environment receptive to approaches from Jack's OUTthere group.

Although Kat's local group has received mixed responses, she acknowledges that groups like WayOut and OUTthere have the advantage of independence in their campaigns, and that 'local government is restricted in [the] level of input they can have with the schools'.

Going hand in hand with organisational independence, however, is organisational risk. OUTthere groups in regional areas must battle some negative press and suspicion from the local community, particularly in locations where young people rarely have a public voice. Jack remarks that 'there are things like Scouts, but as for groups that are run by young people for young people, in my area I'm pretty sure we're the only one ... I don't think a lot of the stuff reaches us [here], it's only if you know the right people who've got their ear to the ground'. Kat, too, finds that her shire 'is very isolating, there's not a lot for young people to do ... the saying [here] is once you turn 18 and get your licence, you're gone'.

The primary project of the OUTthere Rural Victorian Youth Council for Sexual Diversity is to gather data to back more formal approaches to government by surveying 400 teachers and students across the state. As Jack explains: 'Ideally we will be recognised as a strong, influential group with strong links to communities around Victoria, and we'll have that kind of backing, that support, and a trusted understanding of gay rights and gay issues to be recognised as a credible body'.

It seems that credibility is already in train. In 2009, Kat was appointed to the Ministerial Youth Advisory Committee to the Victorian Minister for Youth Affairs, representing OUTthere. A major win for her was to guarantee a saved seat on the council for a representative of the LGBT (lesbian, gay, bisexual, transgender) youth community, even after her time there comes to an end.

Shona Cools: Linkz

> I don't know whether there's necessarily a resistance to getting involved in formal Politics or government per se. I think though that the way that we've been brought up is very much about doing things in the most efficient and effective way possible, which in many cases often leads people outside of that government setting.
>
> (Shona Cools)

When Shona Cools established Linkz Incorporated, a non-profit organisation seeking to foster connections between Indigenous and non-Indigenous Australians, she brought with her several years of experience in federal government. Based in Darwin in the Northern Territory, she had visited dozens of remote communities to discuss housing and welfare and was continually struck by the message that young people needed more to do:

> Particularly during school holiday time, many communities ... effectively empty out, so people like teachers, doctors, nurses, police, council staff all head home and leave the community pretty much on their own for six to eight weeks over the summer holidays, and four to five weeks over the mid-year break ... It's the peak [time] for suicides across the country; it can be an incredibly challenging time to have all of the services removed ... it just didn't make a whole lot of sense.

Though Shona repeatedly communicated her findings, she found that 'it wasn't necessarily getting actioned because it didn't fit within the frameworks of what government was already trying to do'. Leaving government and joining the non-profit sector was a very deliberate move to address the problem. Through Linkz, Shona set up the Remote Community Holiday Program (RCHP), tapping into her own networks of young people who were eager to explore the Northern Territory and learn more about Indigenous culture. These young volunteers are organised into teams that travel to remote communities during school holidays to facilitate sport and recreation programs. They are equipped with accredited training in sport and recreation, first aid and four-wheel driving, and complete an induction program that incorporates community-specific cultural awareness and is run by a local person.

Cooperation with local government has been central to the success of her organisation, but the relationship with higher levels of government can be frustrating. While Linkz works well with shire councils and local governments, Shona explains that state or national departments do not necessarily recognise its work as a priority. At the same time, the broad reach and solid reputation of Linkz Incorporated has made it 'a bit of a go-to', bringing Shona and her team to the notice of government bodies hungry for ground-level information about remote communities.

Linkz members are regularly called in to government consultations, particularly in relation to the federal youth portfolio:

> Our main perspective is putting the issues and the concerns of remote Indigenous youth across, and so while we never speak for them, it's great to have the opportunity to at least make sure that people remember that they're there and that they have some fairly unique challenges and some fairly unique issues.

(Shona Cools)

One member of the Linkz team now sits on the Australian Youth Forum Steering Committee, although this is not always seen as a good thing. At times, Shona says, 'rather than doing proper consultation and checking more broadly, it does appear a little bit like more of a box-ticking exercise'. Shona herself was asked to join the 2020 Youth Summit. The Summit was held at Parliament House in Canberra in April 2008, with 100 youth delegates invited to discuss future directions in education and training, economic infrastructure, population, health, climate change and government:

From the perspective of bringing a whole lot of young people together, who [were] passionate about the different areas they were focused on, it was an incredible experience. In terms of making any sort of difference, of having the ability to set any sort of agenda, that was a fairly tokenistic process I'd say … The parameters of what we were able to address were actually deliberately set.

Progress may be slow, but Shona has observed 'in probably the last four or five years a massive difference in government's willingness to listen. I suppose the key challenge now is for them to learn how to actually take that information and put it into their processes and action it'. In the meantime, the organisation is finding greater strength through community partnerships. In one remote community, for example, which is home to large numbers of gang fighters, Linkz has identified a number of boys who have shown leadership potential and partnered each with a player from the Essendon Football Club, who offer football training and mentoring.

Shona Cools is an example of a young person who has worked within and beyond formal government structures to generate real social change. She attributes her approach to the characteristics of her generation:

I definitely think the Gen Y group, we don't necessarily have the same barriers of questioning the status quo, and also questioning people who are older and who have gone before. I know my parents for example would be a lot more reluctant to do that. The way that we've been brought up means that that's not really an issue. If we can see a better way of doing it, or something's not working properly, there's no hesitation in seeing if we can do something.

References

Interview with **Jack Hegarty** (Barbara Lemon), 13 January 2010.
Interview with **Kathryn Ettwell** (Barbara Lemon), 14 January 2010.
Interview with **Shona Cools** (Barbara Lemon), 14 January 2010.

Commentary 1:
Exclusion, marginalisation and active citizenship

Lucas Walsh

Introduction

The previous viewpoint and case studies describe young people who, to varying extents, feel marginalised and alienated from current political processes and institutions but who are keen to make change. The case studies further illustrate innovative ways that young people are leading change to foster greater inclusion of marginalised groups. They all suggest a need to improve how young people experience belonging in contemporary society, and signal a need to enable and foster better ways for them to actively engage in shaping their worlds. At a fundamental level, these examples speak of an underlying need to better articulate what citizenship means for young people in Australia.

Just over a decade ago, the Australian Citizenship Council (ACC) asked: How can concepts of citizenship best serve Australians (ACC, 2000)? Today, active citizenship is a key component of the *Melbourne Declaration on Educational Goals for Young Australians*, according to which all young Australians should 'become successful learners, confident and creative individuals, and active and informed citizens' (MCEETYA, 2008, p. 7). Signed by all Australian education ministers, the Declaration is a touchstone that links the educational success of young people to a participatory notion of citizenship. 'Active and informed citizens' are those who:
- 'are committed to national values of democracy, equity and justice, and participate in Australia's civic life;
- are able to relate to and communicate across cultures, especially the cultures and countries of Asia;
- work for the common good, in particular sustaining and improving natural and social environments; and
- are responsible global and local citizens' (MCEETYA, 2008, p. 9).

But while much effort is spent on attempting to develop, define and measure educational success, what of active citizenship? Citizenship beyond its legal status is poorly defined, particularly in relation to the lived experience of young people.

This commentary investigates the nature of citizenship and its relevance to the needs, environment and experience of young people in Australia. Enabling people to actively participate in democratic life is vital to democracy. The quality and extent of any given person's participation in the development and decision-making processes of a community will depend on the nature and quality of that person's membership within it. But young people's experiences of marginalisation and exclusion demand a more complex conceptualisation and realisation of citizenship that is more than a legal status and which has been equated with values and historical notions that appear alien to many young people. The following discussion looks at how alienation, exclusion and marginalisation are experienced in political, social, cultural and economic domains of young people's lives.

There is a dissonance between the idea of active citizenship and the reality of young people's experience of full membership, belonging and participation in Australian society. This dissonance takes place both at the level of policy, according to which a narrow definition of social inclusion places primacy of economic concerns over other dimensions of citizenship, right through to everyday life. Young people experience exclusion in a variety of ways, such as alienation from political decision-making, racism, lack of economic mobility and other forms of prejudice. Schooling and education in general recur throughout this discussion of marginalisation and active citizenship as key sites in which exclusion takes place but which also offer potential contexts in which these challenges can be addressed. A deeper analysis of schooling takes place in Chapter 2.

It is from this dissonance that conflicting messages are sent to young people about their membership, status and the value of their participation. We need to clarify and better articulate what is meant by active citizenship in a way that better connects with young people, and which provides a basis for full membership of society. This requires the resources, rights and means necessary to ensure this full membership is a basis upon which active participation becomes possible. Better understanding and articulation of what is meant by active citizenship provides a way of projecting what membership, belonging and connectedness looks like, and how it can better form a basis for enabling young people to make change.

A brief overview of citizenship

In Australia, citizenship is often associated with the formal status of nationality and the laws and rules which govern this status.

During its first 50 years, the legal status of Australian citizenship was also linked to planned migration: namely, the process of naturalisation of over three million migrants who came to Australia after World War II. 'In this sense,' one advisory council suggests, 'the inclusive nature of Australian Citizenship has been spectacularly successful' (ACC, 2000, p. 4). As we will find during this commentary, the evidence indicates that beneath this view, the experience of inclusion by young people reflects a far less inclusive reality.

Beyond the legal status, citizenship further encompasses the quality of full membership and active participation in a just, democratic and mutually supportive community. Sociologist T. H. Marshall (1964, p. 84) defines citizenship as:

> *a status bestowed on those who are full members of a community. All who possess the status are equal with respect to the rights and duties with which the status is endowed. There is no universal principle that determines what those rights and duties shall be, but societies in which citizenship is a developing institution create an image of an ideal citizenship against which achievement can be measured and towards which aspiration can be directed.*

Active participation is necessary for democratic citizenship, and requires as its foundation the conditions for citizens to enjoy full membership. This includes collective and individual rights and responsibilities that go with membership across legal, social, economic, cultural, political and environmental aspects of life.

The evidence suggests that there are deep fissures between the idea of citizenship and the lived experience of belonging to Australian society. During this discussion, I argue for the development of a concept of citizenship which: (1) reflects the lived experience of young people across political, civil, economic and cultural aspects of life; (2) is underpinned by a more sophisticated and representative notion of 'inclusion' than is currently used in Australia; and (3) emphasises the importance of active participation by young people in decision- and change-making across a range of levels and contexts. The scope and capacity for effective participation is defined by the degree to which (1) and (2) are articulated and enjoyed as part of the lived experience of young people as Australian and global citizens.

The following section examines some of the political, cultural and economic ways that young people experience marginalisation, exclusion and alienation from contemporary life. How and in what ways do these take place?

Membership for whom?

Political disengagement and civic deficit

Debates over the nature and quality of citizenship in Australia are perennial and vary in approach. In 1989, a Senate Standing Committee review of student knowledge and understanding of civics and citizenship identified several dangers to democracy, including: apathy and fatalism amongst voters; a lack of civics education; poor awareness of citizenship among young people; and deepening inequalities resulting in increasing numbers of alienated and excluded people with no belief in democracy. The Committee expressed concern that significant levels of ignorance amongst students of civics, history and institutions were conducive to cynicism and apathy (Senate Standing Committee on Employment, Education and Training, 1989). Mackay (1993, p. 25) also observed a loss of direction and isolation in young people. Noting 'some decline in civic values as evidenced by marked increases in the sense of personal alienation, powerlessness and a diminished sense of community', another Senate Committee several years later concluded that 'these circumstances suggest the need for some reappraisal of citizenship, national identity and community goals' (Salvaris, 1995, p. 6). Other research during the 1990s indicated 'a profoundly inadequate civic understanding by Australian youth' according to which 'even the most basic of political and parliamentary processes appear to be unknown to most Australian students' (Print, 1995). One influential advisory team, the Civics Expert Group (CEG), described it in terms of 'civic deficit' (CEG, 1994).

Acknowledging the problem of civic deficit and a need to reinvigorate political life in general, the possibility of a Bill of Rights was also raised during the 1990s, proposals for which continue to this day. There was also considerable discussion about the need to better articulate the goals and values of Australian citizenship and how these could be monitored through benchmarks and indicators (Hattam, 1995). Perhaps most influential during the latter 1990s was the 'strong surge of interest in how concepts of citizenship can be a focal point for the civic values that form the central framework of Australia's democratic society and can provide a strong unifying element. This was seen as having particular importance in Australia's increasingly multicultural society where traditional national symbols have somewhat less relevance as Australia seeks to find its place in the 21st century' (ACC, 2000, p. 4).

Civics and citizenship education was identified as a means of addressing civic deficit and promoting citizenship as a unifying symbol. This sparked the development of a series of civics and citizenship educational resources entitled 'Discovering Democracy'. This ambitious program was 'premised on the conviction that civics and citizenship education is central to Australian education and the maintenance of a strong and vital citizenship' (Curriculum Corporation, 2009). Building a thorough knowledge and understanding of Australia's democratic processes and government, political heritage and judicial system was advocated as the basis for improving citizenship, participation and engagement.

The Centenary of Federation presented further opportunities to explore how democracy could be strengthened (Centenary of Federation Advisory Committee, 1994). The 1998 Australian Constitutional Convention to determine whether Australia should become a republic stimulated further reflection and dialogue around citizenship and identity. The Australian Citizenship Council suggested 'a wider concept of citizenship, that is, membership of the Australian community and adherence to civic values which unite us – whether a person is an Australian Citizen or not. This has not really been a central focus of Australian consciousness, at least not under the label of "citizenship"' (ACC, 2000, p. 4). In 2006, one of the themes to emerge from the 100 or so submissions to a parliamentary inquiry into Civics and Electoral Education was the need to explore how young people can be enabled to engage and participate more in democratic life (Joint Standing Committee on Electoral Matters, 2006). An inquiry into the machinery of referendums three years later asked the same question (House of Representatives Standing Committee on Legal and Constitutional Affairs, 2009).

A major review entitled the *State of Australia's Young People* published in 2009 provides an excellent snapshot of young people's current civic participation (Muir et al., 2009). Young people's civic engagement occurs in three ways: through community participation, through electoral activity (participation in campaigns and elections), and through expressing opinions on issues of concern. Participation by young people in these civic activities is comparatively low and often irregular. One in three young people aged 19 to 24 participate in civic activities, such as voting (Muir et al., 2009). In 2004, only 82 per cent of young people (aged 17 to 25) were on the electoral roll compared with 95 per cent of other Australians (AEC, 2007). Despite concerted efforts to address this disparity, in 2008 roughly one in five eligible 18–25 year olds were still not enrolled to vote (Australian Government, 2009). Disadvantage and marginalisation appear to be related to low levels of enrolment by young people, as well as civic disengagement. Similarly, young people who are Indigenous, culturally and linguistically diverse (CALD), living in low socio-economic circumstances, or have a disability are not widely engaged in decision-making processes (Muir et al., 2009).

Patterns of civic participation in Australia indicate that younger people engage significantly less in activities such as volunteering and voting in comparison to older age groups. Data from 2006 indicates that older people, for example, were more likely to participate in civic activities (General Social Survey, 2006, cited in Muir et al., 2009). The proportion of young people who volunteer on a regular basis is also low. Those young people who volunteer do so for a range of reasons, such as personal satisfaction, helping the community, as well as for family reasons. Levels of civic participation appear to be related to engagement in other areas of life such as work and study. Educated young people are, for example, more likely to participate in civic life (Muir et al., 2009). Those who complete school, unlike those who haven't completed school, are more likely to be engaged in community activities and are more likely to say that living in a democracy is very important to them (World Values Survey Association, 2009; Lamb, Robinson & Walstab, 2010). Those in paid work also exhibit greater propensity to volunteer for community-based civic activities than young people not engaged in study or employment. Age, socio-economic status and geographic location also impact on young people's propensity and capacity to volunteer (Muir et al., 2009). There continues to be concern that many Australians experience apathy, lack of confidence in political affairs, personal alienation, powerlessness and exclusion from civic life. Young people, it has been repeatedly noted, are of particular concern (Salvaris, 1995).

Cultural exclusion and marginalisation

Surprisingly, for a country so profoundly shaped by its Indigenous heritage, migration, and flows of knowledge, goods and services, the importance of cultural diversity remains poorly articulated in the lexicon of modern Australian citizenship. Australians aged 12 to 24 years comprise a culturally and linguistically diverse group of people. More diverse than any other age group, they embody a society whose fabric is woven from the global movement of people, encompassing everything from tourism and modern migration dating back through convict settlement to the origins of the first Australians. Today, young Australians who were born overseas make up one-fifth of the total population aged 12 to 24. One in five speaks a language other than English at home. Indigenous young people account for 3.6 per cent of young people aged 15 to 19 and just under three per cent of all people aged 20 to 24 (Muir et al., 2009, p. 12). These trends reflect the reality that to be a young person in Australia is to be part of a diverse society.

Cultural differences shape and impact young people in a variety of ways. For some, it is a source of pride, belonging and identity. For others, practices of exclusion based on cultural differences impact upon their sense of belonging in negative ways and can profoundly shape how young people participate in economic, social and political life. The language spoken at home can impact upon how a young person interacts with their families. Differences in gender roles between cultures can impact on the status and expectations of young women (Francis & Cornfoot, 2007). Too many young people experience some form of racism.

Defined broadly as an exclusionary 'set of practices and discourses' (Castles, 1996, p. 31), the experience of racism appears to be prevalent amongst young people. A survey commissioned by The Foundation for Young Australians of 823 students aged 12 to 19 years found that students from migrant backgrounds were most likely to experience racist behaviour. Those who had been in Australia less than five years were six times more likely to experience some form of racism, ranging from negative comments relating to their cultural background, to physically threatening behaviour. While young Indigenous Australians reported fewer racist incidents than their peers from migrant backgrounds, qualitative data derived from interviews suggests a more pervasive experience of racism in everyday life (Mansouri et al., 2009). Another study of youth attitudes to racism found that people aged 18 to 24 who were not born in Australia were almost twice as likely to experience intolerance and discrimination as those born in Australia (Forrest, 2009).

For many, exclusion begins at an early age and for some the physical and psychological impact is significant (VicHealth, 2009). Young women from migrant backgrounds are amongst the worst affected (Mansouri et al., 2009).

Many young people who experience racism take no action in response. Lack of trust is one key reason. Robert, a boy born in Montenegro, describes one impact of racism in Australia: 'All I know is I don't trust no-one, even if you're my closest friend, I trust my dad and my mum and my two sisters, but I don't trust no-one. Cause everyone can do the dirty on you, so I don't trust no-one' (Mansouri et al., 2009, p. 80). Mansouri and colleagues' (2009) survey found that just over half would report racism to a teacher, while less than a third approached their school counsellor. Twelve per cent reported it to police with a small number seeking the advice of a health professional. This suggests a potentially deeper, systemic experience of marginalisation and prejudice.

The isolating effects of racism may be compounded by a trend in young people born overseas who do not speak English at home to spend less time with family than those born overseas who speak English at home, or who were born in Australia (Muir et al., 2009). Francis and Cornfoot (2007, cited in Muir et al., 2009) suggest that this may be linked to young people from migrant and refugee backgrounds who have experienced family disruption and isolation from members of their families.

The experience of exclusion by young people is consequently played out within a complex dynamic of identity, culture, demography, gender, family and institutions, such as school and the police. The diversity and attitude of young people resist simple categorisations of what is actually 'included' or 'excluded'. For example, while 80 per cent of students from non-Anglo backgrounds have been subjected to some form of racism, 55 per cent of young people from Anglo-Australian backgrounds also experience racism (Mansouri et al., 2009). Furthermore, research by Forrest (2009) found that while younger Australians aged 18 to 24 are more accepting than the overall population of aspects of multiculturalism such as inter-racial marriage, just over a quarter of those surveyed indicated a belief that some groups do not 'fit' into Australian society. Manifest in a variety of forms, racism is thus often based on a 'contradictory set of assumptions by which people understand and cope with the social worlds in which they live' (Castles, cited in Mansouri et al., 2009, p. 12).

Some racist practices and discourses are entwined with the development of the nation-state and the nature of membership to it. The period of White Australia policies (1901 to the mid-1970s), for example, was characterised by a regulation and restriction of 'non-white' immigration to Australia. Aside from enforcing overt practices of racial demarcation and exclusion based on colour, a secondary effect of this was to entrench differences between migrants with the legal status of Australian citizenship from those who do not have this status (such as refugees). '[D]eeply rooted in the history, traditions and culture of modernity', Stephen Castles writes, practices and discourses of racism play 'a crucial role in consolidating nation-states, by providing an instrument for defining belonging or exclusion' (Castles, 1996, p. 31). But they are also bound up with globalisation beyond the nation-state in ways that have been intensified by contemporary developments in areas such as information and communication technology.

The lack of recognition of the benefits and challenges of diversity is evident in other aspects of young people's lives, such as those who are same sex attracted. Around one in ten young Australians experience same sex attraction (Hillier, Turner & Mitchell, 2005). The marginalisation and abuse of young gay, lesbian, bisexual, transgender, intersex (GLBTI) people often has similar effects to racism on wellbeing. Victims of homophobic violence and emotional abuse may experience anxiety, depression and thoughts of self-harm and suicide. Those with a history of verbal, sexual and/or physical abuse and victimisation are at greater risk than heterosexual young people of higher levels of social and mental health problems (Lock & Steiner, 1999).

Over the last three decades, same sex attraction has become increasingly accepted as a normal part of diverse society. Formal recognition is also evident in the form of greater health and legal services and support for same sex attracted couples, and the acceptance of young GLBTI people into some faith-based institutions. Despite these positive developments, a stigmatisation of homosexuality is still pervasive. Many students who are known to be same sex attracted experience isolation and bullying at school. A study published in 2005 found that 44 per cent of young non-heterosexual people experienced verbal abuse, while 16 per cent reported physical abuse (Hillier, Turner & Mitchell, 2005). The complex challenges and potentially rich benefits of diversity demand a more rigorous and nuanced understanding of citizenship.

Social inclusion and economic marginalisation

Recent policy narratives of social inclusion place high importance on the economic benefits of making smooth transitions from school to work or further study and training. An explicit target group of current policy is 'working families'. The marginalisation of young people from these opportunities is related to factors such as economic instability, background, location, demographic change and long-term labour market trends that work against young people.

The vulnerability of young people to economic instability was particularly evident in the wake of the global financial crisis (GFC). While Australians overall fared comparatively well, the same could not be said for many young people, who were affected immediately and disproportionately as a result of the 2008 downturn (Robinson & Lamb, 2009; Lamb, Robinson & Walstab, 2010). This impact was felt by many young people throughout the world, particularly in the United States (Organisation for Economic Co-operation & Development, 2009).

Before the GFC, unemployment for young people aged 15 to 24 was at the lowest recorded level since the 1970s (Organisation for Economic Co-operation & Development, 2009). This low level of unemployment was in part due to greater numbers of young people choosing to study or undertake training before entering the workforce (Lamb & Mason, 2008; Lamb Robinson & Walstab, 2010). Youth unemployment then climbed significantly in 2009 (Robinson & Lamb, 2009). Teenagers in particular felt the effects of the downturn more acutely than many other members of the workforce. In Australia, unemployment rates are much higher for teenagers in comparison to the population (aged 15–64) as a whole (Lamb, Robinson & Walstab, 2010). The sharp rise in the percentage of teenagers not fully engaged reflected similar trends in disengagement experienced at the time of the 1990s recession.

Young men in apprenticeships were among the first to be affected (Organisation for Economic Co-operation & Development, 2009; Robinson & Lamb, 2009). Fewer teenagers began apprenticeships in 2009, the level of commencements having stalled and then decreased following the GFC. With the significant increase in the percentage of teenagers not fully engaged in 2009, there was no significant offsetting increase in educational participation.

In addition to the vulnerability of working young people to economic instability, longer-term trends in the labour force suggest that full-time job opportunities for teenagers are becoming scarcer. Despite over 10 years of uninterrupted economic growth prior to the GFC, there were few gains in full-time opportunities for young people. In recent years, decreasing full-time job opportunities for teenagers have been offset to some extent by an increase in participation in full-time education (Walsh, 2010). As casual and part-time work becomes increasingly common in young teenagers' lives, so too it appears to be more frequent in the late teens. Amongst those in part-time work, recent evidence suggests that many women aged 18–19 would prefer to work more but do not have opportunities to do so (Pocock, Skinner & Pisaniello, 2010). A labour market that is hostile to many young women appears to be driving them to shelter in education (Lamb, Robinson & Walstab, 2010).

Location plays a critical role in shaping the social inclusion of young people as they move from school to work and further study or training. Attainment of qualifications post-school varies according to where young people live. Those with no school qualifications by the age of 24 (around 55 per cent) are most likely to be living in the least advantaged areas, in contrast to the wealthiest areas where only 30 per cent have no post-school qualifications by the age of 24 (Robinson & Lamb, 2009). Employment opportunities increasingly require higher levels of qualifications (for example, see Foster et al., 2007). The type of qualification young people attain also varies according to where they live. In 2006, 46 per cent of young people living in the wealthiest areas had a university degree by the age of 24 as compared to only 14 per cent in the poorest areas (Robinson & Lamb, 2009). Hence, where a young person lives has significant implications for their experience of social inclusion.

Too many Indigenous young Australians face particularly intense challenges. But on the positive side, the rate of participation of Indigenous young people in full-time education, particularly in school, has increased in relative and absolute terms in recent years. Participation in full-time employment also increased during the last decade. The proportion of young Indigenous adults who completed year 12 and attained post-school qualifications grew substantially as well. However, participation in full-time study by young Indigenous adults and 25–29 year olds has shown signs of stagnation and decline. Rates of attainment of higher education qualifications have not significantly grown despite increasing levels of year 12 completion. The rate of year 12 or equivalent completion is about half that of non-Indigenous young people (Long & North, 2009). The proportion of non-Indigenous people aged 25–29 with degrees is six times higher than Indigenous young people. Achievement levels of Indigenous students in areas such as literacy and year 12 completion remain unacceptably low compared to non-Indigenous students (Lamb, Robinson & Walstab, 2010). There are a range of complex reasons for this, including geographical isolation, lack of family and community support, and the absence of clear pathways and fewer opportunities for those living in remote communities to earn and learn. In addition, trends indicating a relatively higher growth of population in Indigenous communities compared to the non-Indigenous population (possibly due to higher birth rates and possibly greater numbers of people identifying as 'Indigenous') has significant implications for higher school participation and completion (Walsh, 2010).

The marginalisation of young people from opportunities to earn and learn has particular implications given their stage of development. Working offers young people economic, social and educational benefits. Aside from the income and professional experience, young people at work can benefit from: the social engagement of their workplace environment; learning about responsibility; and increased self-esteem from securing financial mobility.

For those who are studying while working, there are also dangers. A Parliamentary Inquiry expressed concern that young people were working too many hours at the risk of compromising their educational outcomes (House of Representatives, 2009).

When we look at trends over the past two decades, we see that opportunities for full-time employment have flattened or not increased alongside Australia's economic growth. The most vulnerable groups, such as teenage males who are not engaged in education, Indigenous young people, those living in remote and regional areas, and young people from disadvantaged backgrounds face particular challenges of marginalisation during a key formative period of their lives. Perhaps most alarmingly, a high number of young people were living in poverty during the economically prosperous years immediately *prior* to the GFC. At the time of the 2006 census, almost one in every 100 young people aged between 12 and 24 was homeless (Muir et al., 2009). A 2009 report by the Australian Human Rights Commission states that 46 per cent of homeless people were younger than 25 (Australian Human Rights Commission, 2009a).

The development of a more robust, engaging and inclusive notion of active citizenship needs to consider the challenges of marginalisation, disengagement and exclusion from the areas of civil, political, cultural and economic life discussed above. (These areas are only some of the contexts in which young people experience disengagement, marginalisation and exclusion. Other significant challenges occur across other areas of life, such as mental and physical health, disability and gender, but are not covered within the scope of this book.) In seeking to respond to the challenges of exclusion and marginalisation, it is useful to understand the types of broad policy responses across the areas of political disengagement and civic deficit, cultural exclusion and economic marginalisation in relation to different dimensions of citizenship.

Policy responses

Responses to political disengagement

Firstly, efforts to improve political disengagement and civic deficit through civics and citizenship education (described in the first section of this commentary) have consistently failed because they have not addressed the distance young people feel from political decision-making, nor have they adequately responded to the challenges of realising what 'full membership' actually looks like. Part of this failure arises from a lack of engagement with the real lives of young people and the ways that they experience exclusion; hence, a connection has not been established with young people. Some of the recent proposals for change raise some key questions, not only about how to improve young people's engagement with civil and political life, but about how their maturity, agency and youth are defined within broader conventional discourses about young people.

One of the suggestions to come out of the 2020 summit in 2008 was to lower the right to vote to age 16 to extend and encourage youth participation. Appealing to the democratic principle that all members of the society have equal access and power, it is argued that there currently exists an inconsistency in how the legal definition of what constitutes maturity is applied across different domains of young people's lives. For example, 16-year-olds are legally considered emotionally and mentally able to consent to sex, but cannot vote on related election issues such as the legalisation of abortion. Sixteen-year-olds can also be considered legally independent and receive welfare, but cannot vote (Warnock, 2008). Implicitly appealing to the question of what constitutes 'full membership' of society, advocates highlight other inconsistencies in the treatment of other forms of participation, such as work. Warnock (2008) argues that a 16-year-old can, for example, work full-time and be taxed according to the laws of a government with which he/she had no hand in electing. The Australian Electoral Commission (AEC) disputes this, arguing that 'just because some rights are acquired at 16 does not mean that other, unrelated, rights should be. We do not ask 16-year-olds to serve in the defence forces or on juries, and we do not allow them to gamble or purchase alcohol and tobacco' (AEC, 2007, p. 72). The AEC's position is that lowering the voting age to 16 will not encourage young people to enrol to vote. It argues (using sweeping generalisations) that 16-year-olds lack a suitable level of maturity to vote and are 'too distracted by adolescent interests to become responsible and informed voters. They are still growing up and need more time to learn about the world before they take on the responsibility of voting. Such learning must come from life experience, not formal education' (AEC, 2007, p. 72). With regards to the last point, one would surely hope that young people draw from both.

At the heart of this argument is that young people with rights and responsibilities on one area should be entitled to rights in another. There is substance to the argument for a kind of balancing of certain social rights (e.g. to welfare and work) with the right to vote. Basing reform on a particular notion of maturity is problematic. A key problem here is that legal definitions of maturity are derived from different disciplines (e.g. health sciences, economic indicators, historical contexts and legal precedents). While some are outdated, there is no single agreed definition of maturity upon which to posit an ideal year to begin voting. What is consistent across this discourse, of civics and citizenship education and schooling more broadly, is an infantilisation of young people. We will explore this infantilisation throughout this book.

Cultural citizenship and responses to cultural exclusion

Turning now to practices and discourses of cultural exclusion and inclusion: greater awareness of cultural diversity, environmental issues and the needs of Indigenous peoples, for example, has led to a need to develop cultural citizenship defined in terms of cultural rights (Delanty, 2000). The idea of cultural citizenship is relatively new and a source of debate amongst scholars (Ommundsen, Leach & Vandenberg, 2010). Miller (2001, p. 2) associates cultural citizenship with 'the maintenance and development of cultural lineage through education, custom, language and religion, and the positive acknowledgement of difference in and by the mainstream'. Turner takes it a step further, describing cultural citizenship in terms of 'cultural empowerment', by which he means 'the capacity to participate effectively, creatively and successfully within a national culture' (Turner in Stevenson, 2003, p. 12). This implies full and equal access to educational institutions, unimpeded use of any living language, and the freedom of people to identify with and socialise their children into a culture. Government recognition of cultural diversity and associated rights, such as the freedom to express one's own culture and freedom from discrimination, is most visible in the shifting policies and programs of multiculturalism.

Multiculturalism has been built on principles, such as the right of all citizens to express their own culture and beliefs and the obligation for them to accept the right of others to do the same, and the right to equality of treatment and opportunity free from discrimination on the grounds of race, culture, religion, language, location, gender or place of birth (Department of Immigration & Citizenship, 2009). Acknowledging these rights represents a more sophisticated notion of citizenship that reflects the profound impact of globalisation in positive and negative ways.

Recognition of cultural rights in government policy has taken place relatively recently. It was mainly sparked by a need for new policy in response to the challenges of post-World War II migration, rather than as an enduring principle, benefit or dimension of citizenship. Lacking the formal weight of constitutional recognition, the acknowledgement of these rights depends on the attitudes of the government of the day. They are further conditional on the basis that citizens can enjoy these rights provided they uphold existing democratic values and traditions (Department of Immigration & Citizenship, 2009).

With its origins in migrant settlement, multiculturalism in Australia began as policy related to accommodating the cultures of first-generation migrants, while encouraging second and third generations to integrate around a set of civic values and norms consistent with Australian citizenship (Walsh & Leach, 2007). A major turning point in Australia began in 1975 with the Whitlam government's termination of White Australia policy (Bradford, 2007). This shift inaugurated a new area of policy and debate about the role and significance of cultural diversity, particularly in relation to immigration. White Australia policies (going back to 1901) had actively restricted 'non-white' immigration to Australia, but by the end of the 1970s policy around migration adopted a more nuanced understanding of those undergoing the settlement process. In contrast to the blunt language of *assimilation* of previous years, this shift signalled a greater awareness of the rights and needs of those from non-Anglo backgrounds. In a major review of migrant services from this period, we can see an emerging recognition of cultural pluralism and the rights of ethnic groups to cultural maintenance, as well as the need for institutional change (Galbally, 1978; Cox, 1996). But this recognition of diversity only extended so far. Cultural rights were recognised as long as they were exercised in a manner consistent with Australian citizenship and adhered to values and institutions. With the evolution and extension of multiculturalism policy over the next two decades (e.g. see Office of Multicultural Affairs, 1989; National Multicultural Advisory

Council, 1995), rights to cultural diversity, social justice and economic inclusion have had the following as their corollary: the obligation that all citizens should have an overriding and unifying commitment to Australia; that all Australians accept the basic democratic structures and principles of Australian society; and to accept the rights of others to express their views and values (Batrouney, 2002).

Again, the implications of this policy flow from cultural citizenship to other domains of life, such as civil participation. For example, even after Indigenous people gained the unqualified right to vote in Commonwealth elections in 1962, enrolment was not compulsory as it was for other citizens. Differentiating the duty and obligation to vote in this way was exclusionary and ran counter to Australia's track record in extending suffrage. It reflected a pervasive attitude according to which voting by Indigenous citizens was not encouraged. A major step forward took place in 1984(!) with the introduction of compulsory enrolment and voting in Commonwealth elections for Indigenous people and the provision of mobile polling to remote areas (AEC, 2006).

Responses to economic marginalisation and exclusion

Current thinking about economic wellbeing is connected to problematic notions of social citizenship and social inclusion. The 'Earn or Learn' agenda of the Rudd and Gillard governments represents a concerted response to the recent challenges of economic instability. This policy attempt to promote smoother transitions from school to work, post-school study and training was part of a broader agenda of social inclusion, with a focus on economic wellbeing and 'working families'.

Commentators and policy-makers often incorrectly associate social rights with socio-economic rights only. The Rudd and Gillard governments' narrative of social inclusion, for example, largely defined social inclusion within a narrow prism of employment and financial security. The idea of social citizenship was reduced to the level of welfare and government-sponsored benefits. The reliance on economic indicators, incentives and definitions to inform the world view is by no means new – Donald Horne noted this shift during the 1990s as traditional notions of national identity began to be replaced by abstract economic concepts and measures (Salvaris, 1995). Implicit in the narrative of social inclusion that has dominated policy is a model of cohesion according to which citizens should assimilate first and then worry about speaking up later. The notion of social inclusion also privileges a limited, economic view of what constitutes exclusion (focused on working families and full-time education) over other areas such as marginalisation based on race or sexual orientation. The notion of social citizenship that dominates current policy approaches to inclusion needs to be challenged and reconsidered in relation to other dimensions of young people's lives, such as the civil, political and cultural areas described above.

Developing a shared vision of active citizenship

What is lacking in these narratives related to citizenship is a common vision of what full membership looks like. A common theme to emerge during the last 20 years in many government, parliamentary and advisory reviews and recommendations is the importance of citizenship's role as a unifying symbol (Australian Citizenship Council, 2000, p. 1). An example is the Australian Citizenship Council's investigation of how concepts of citizenship can best serve Australia and Australians. Arguing that 'more can be made of citizenship' beyond a legal status, the Council focused on the symbolic role of citizenship and the importance of shared values to add meaning. Building on two key reports from 1994, *Australians all – Enhancing Australian citizenship* (Joint Standing Committee on Migration, 1994) and *Whereas the people …* (Civics Expert Group, 1994), the Council recommended that 'the primary focus should be on Australian citizenship as involving certain widely held but often unexpressed civic values rather than simply on the legal status of Citizenship. These civic values, having evolved over time, already form the foundation of Australia's democratic society', and 'if appropriately promoted throughout the community they will give added meaning to Australian citizenship' (Australian Citizenship Council, 2000, p. 1). Citizenship 'provides a unifying theme that is based on values widely accepted in the Australian community, such as democracy, fairness, tolerance, participation and social solidarity … [A]n enriched citizenship may be the key to keeping a diverse and multicultural society together' (Salvaris, 1995, p. 10).

Citizenship should be grounded in a set of values and moral qualities. While there is no universal principle that determines what particular rights and duties shall be with regards to the status of full membership, 'societies in which citizenship is a developing institution', Marshall writes, 'create an image of an ideal citizenship against which achievement can be measured and towards which aspiration can be directed' (Marshall, 1964, p. 84). Given the diversity of young people, a key question is: what values are common to all? And returning to the *Melbourne Declaration*, what does active citizenship look like in practice and how does this relate to the lived experience of young people?

Articulating what active citizenship looks like must incorporate new and emergent ways of change-making that form 'a vibrant stratum of the population that is outstripping older peers in terms of innovative democratic engagement' (Banaji, 2008, p. 544). The case studies of Kat, Jack and Shona provide insight into three areas of this discussion. Firstly, they reflect the attitudes of many young people who feel varying degrees of alienation from mainstream political participation. Secondly, they provide examples of how young people are seeking alternative pathways to influence and engage change. Thirdly, all three are in one way or another addressing the needs of people experiencing exclusion, ranging from advocating for same sex attracted young people in rural Victoria, to connecting remote Indigenous and non-Indigenous youth. They reflect types of participation that sit outside conventional discourses of participation and provide insight into how we can better understand how young people are making change. Further examples of these are explored in Chapter 3 of this book.

Developing a consistent language about youth

A controversial view is put forward by Banaji (2008), who questions whether conventional forms of civic and political engagement, such as voting or supporting a political party, are in fact benign and desirable goals for young people. Much of the literature around youth, policy and civic engagement, Banaji argues, treats the 'political' as 'primarily configured as pertaining to elections and government', and 'civic' as the 'implicitly pro-social and conformist field within which future citizens are educated for political engagement'. Challenging the notion of 'civic engagement under any circumstances as an unquestionable good', she presents the possibility that in disengaging, young people may be voting with their feet. She provocatively asks whether it is in fact the political system that is inherently flawed. Deliberate disengagement from the political system may be a political act in itself. To some extent, this resonates with the feelings of alienation described by Kat and Jack from OUTthere. But these social pioneers have pursued other paths to engage, participate in community development and make change to support a more inclusive society. The capacity for young people to lead change depends on a belief that their contribution and voice is valued (at any level). These suggest that we need to challenge inherent assumptions about the capacity of systems to enable young people to make change, decide how to alter these systems, and identify how young people are making change in new ways.

In focusing on a deficit view of young people's experience of political disengagement, much of the discussion about civic deficit and alienation from civic involvement has failed to take account of the ways that young people do seek to make change. Furthermore, the frustration expressed by the young people from the case studies, as well as by the young people discussed in James Arvanitakis and Eric Sidoti's viewpoint, reflects a deeper problem in which discourses about young people are inconsistent, biased and serve to distance them from participation in cultural, economic, political and civil life.

In the political domain, for example, the approach of the Australian Electoral Commission (AEC) to young people's capacity to vote (cited above) relies on an exclusive definition of maturity according to which teenagers are seen to be in transition ('still growing up') to an adult entitlement (and 'responsibility') to vote. Implying that young people are 'distracted', 'irresponsible' and 'uninformed', is not only patronising but serves to stifle, undermine and marginalise their sense of agency. In doing so, this discourse infantilises young people through patronising language and lack of direct consultation.

In suggesting that young people require life experience rather than formal education to be able to vote responsibly, the AEC further devalues their capacities while relegating them to the sidelines until they reach the arbitrary age at which they are viewed as adults. This type of discourse about young people derails their agency by treating the 'teen' years as a transitional stage on the way to adulthood rather than a period in which young people are already active agents in their own lives.

Contemporary understandings of social citizenship and social policy reveal similar problems. The notion of 'successful transition' from school to work and/or further study is often equated unproblematically to improved wellbeing overall. While the evidence suggests that there are clear links between completion of schooling and better health and sense of agency (Lamb, Robinson & Walstab, 2010), Wyn (2010) has suggested that the labour market policies developed during the 1990s based on this assumption around transitions may have had a detrimental effect by not taking into consideration the broader range of factors contributing to wellbeing.

The point is that underpinning the development of active citizenship needs to be a consistent and evidence-based language around youth, their agency and wellbeing. The articulation of active citizenship also needs to be supported by the recognition of the rights and resources necessary for its ongoing realisation.

The role of rights and education

One way of seriously exploring a basis for institutional systemic change in favour of a deeper model of inclusion is through the formalisation of a Bill of Rights. While some states have established charters and bills of rights, the need to establish a more formal national recognition of rights has been the subject of debate for some time. Australia is one of a few Western democracies without an explicit enumeration of its citizens' rights. A Bill of Rights can fulfil a number of important roles in relation to democratic citizenship. It can articulate core shared values, such as equality and respect. Rights have as their corollary a duty on the part of citizens 'to respect the enjoyment of rights by others' (Salvaris, 1995, p. 14). Because they sit outside the jurisdiction of a country's legislative body, rights also provide a means to check the abuse of government power. But some critics argue that to place authority and responsibility for the Bill of Rights in the hands of unelected judges also risks abuse and runs counter to the principle of electoral representation (e.g. see Howard, 2009).

It is argued that children and young people are particularly vulnerable due to a lack of sufficient human rights protection. The Australian Human Rights Commission provides the example of young people who are often 'moved on' from public places where they gather, under laws which give police broad powers to 'move on' or detain people in public spaces. These powers disproportionately impact on young people, especially Indigenous and homeless youth. Many children in Australia are subjected to child abuse and neglect or are exposed to domestic violence. Others are not able to access adequate educational opportunities, particularly in rural and remote areas (Australian Human Rights Commission, 2009b, p. 17).

The role of a Bill of Rights in providing protection against the abuse of power by political representatives is a necessary basis for enshrining the conditions for democratic citizenship. Australia is worse off for lacking this critical legal and symbolic anchor, with direct implications for young people.

Beyond the use of rights as a legal and symbolic framework for articulating the scope and nature of full membership, the realisation of active citizenship also depends on the availability of public and private policies and resources to sustain it (Salvaris, 1995, pp. 5–6).

As we shall see in following chapters, while the role of schooling in shaping citizenship and participation has been problematic, it can nevertheless play a significant role in fostering active citizenship. As stated above, recent attempts to reinvigorate civics and citizenship education have consistently failed to connect with the real lives of young people. They have drawn from conventional notions of citizenship that have relied on looking both backwards (to history) and inwards (to pre-existing institutions and values) (Davidson, 1997). As the last major attempt to introduce and reinvigorate civics and citizenship education, Discovering Democracy did not succeed for similar reasons. One reason was that the units placed too much emphasis on the historical component of civics and citizenship education at the expense of other forms of knowledge and learning both necessary to, and resulting from, active participation. Davidson suggests that the Civics Experts Group 'confused civics education with learning history ... which perpetuated the myth of a highly democratic citizenry at the creation of the Constitution and its practical expression' (Davidson, 1997, pp. 141–142).

Nevertheless, the completion of school is linked to the realisation of active citizenship in key ways. Young people who have a sense of where they want to go after leaving school tend to fare better in the transition to work and further study. Those who complete school have a greater sense of control over their lives in comparison to those who drop out early. International data affirms the importance of finishing school to the confidence of young people and their experience of citizenship. They are more likely to participate in community organisations and be engaged in voluntary community work. They also see living in a democracy as important. Their wellbeing across a range of indicators improves. They are more likely to fulfil the goal of the *Melbourne Declaration* as active citizens, not just locally, but with a global perspective in mind (Lamb, Robinson & Walstab, 2010).

Conclusion

For active citizenship to be a core feature of a just and mutually supportive political community (Kukathas, Lovell & Maley, 1990), all citizens should, as a minimum requirement, have equal opportunities to exercise their rights as well as the duties, obligations and responsibilities that come with full civic membership. The citizen 'believes in the concept of democratic society and has the capacity and desire to translate this belief into action' (Senate Standing Committee on Employment, Education and Training, 1989). As James Arvanitakis and Eric Sidoti suggest, a fundamental challenge for Australian democracy is to open the doors to young people in a way that recognises and supports their capacity for enacted citizenship across political, cultural, economic and other spheres of life. These range from the expectation to participate in voting, to the duty to respect the values of others, to the obligation to participate economically in a variety of ways. Moreover, as the viewpoint and case studies suggest, an articulation of active citizenship will need to encompass the diverse ways that young people seek to engage with and participate in shaping their world.

Throughout this commentary, I have explored ways that young people experience exclusion and marginalisation across civil, economic and cultural domains of life. Factors such as educational attainment, working situation and socio-economic status are related to the level of participation by young people (Muir et al., 2009). Certain cultural backgrounds and low socio-economic status are often linked to disengagement by young people from volunteer activities, voting and decision-making in general. Young people at particular risk of marginalisation live in regional and remote areas, come from low socio-economic status backgrounds and leave school before year 12.

Evidence of widespread racism suggests that too many young people experience exclusion. The experiences described above of intolerance, marginalisation and exclusion of young people suggest social and cultural divisions between how young people themselves define political membership and duties to respect the views and heritage of others. Despite the profound role of cultural diversity in shaping Australian society, recognition of cultural rights has been minimal, erratic, and often rhetorical or attached to transient policy. Some states have been far more active than recent federal governments in promoting cultural diversity as a central component of democratic life (Walsh & Leach, 2007). More needs to be done at a national level.

A Bill of Rights could play an important role both symbolically in explicitly articulating the values, standards and duties of respect, and by providing a check to potential abuses of government power. 'Rights', Putnam wryly observes, 'are the prized possessions of alienated persons' (Putnam, cited in Campbell, 1983, p. 8). But such a Bill could provide an invaluable symbolic and legal foundation upon which full membership could be developed for all people as a basis for a more dynamic and inclusive conception of active citizenship. Recognition of diversity is further possible by extending opportunities for political participation, deliberation and voices to be heard through democratic public spaces. Education can play a powerful role in this, as will be discussed in Chapter 2.

Social, family, economic, cultural and political factors impact young people's experience of full membership and, consequently, their capacity to participate in shaping their world. Young people's mixed experiences of belonging, inclusion and participation resist conventional categories and suggest a need to reflect and better articulate what Australian citizenship means and how it relates to young people's sense of global citizenship. They compel us to rethink and redefine citizenship to better foster, protect and inspire the realisation of full membership. Feelings of belonging and identity formation are fluid and heterogeneous. Citizens are, as James and Eric suggest, 'no longer stable, homogenised, nor bound to a single nation and place'. As the concerns and lifestyles of young people increasingly become enmeshed in the global, the development of active citizenship advocated in this discussion will need to incorporate both local and global experiences of belonging and membership.

While the importance of young Australians is explicitly identified in government and policy narratives such as the *Melbourne Declaration*, the voice of young people continues to be largely absent in contributing to the articulation and implementation of these goals. What do young people believe to be in their best interests? How do young people define success in study, work and life and how would they like it to be measured? These remain important but unanswered questions. While there have been significant advances in consulting young people, more needs to be done. This will also be discussed later in this book.

A deep and potentially challenging national discussion about citizenship that actively includes and values the contributions of young people not only creates a shared vision of active citizenship, but also equips them with a powerful language of possibility – a possibility for young people to feel included and valued, to participate in Australia's political, social and economic development, to make change where necessary and, as active citizens, to lead happy and healthy lives.

References

Australian Citizenship Council (ACC). (2000). *Australian citizenship for a new century: A report by the Australian Citizenship Council, February 2000*. Canberra: Commonwealth of Australia.

Australian Electoral Commission (AEC). (2006). *History of the Indigenous vote.* Canberra: Commonwealth of Australia. Retrieved 10 April 2010 from: http://www.aec.gov.au/pdf/education/resources/history_indigenous_vote.pdf

Australian Electoral Commission (AEC). (2007). *Young people and the vote.* Retrieved 22 February 2010 from: http://www.aec.gov.au/Education/Democracy_Rules/files/Blackline_Masters/Topic3_BLM02.pdf

Australian Government. (2009). *Electoral Reform Green Paper: Strengthening Australia's democracy.* Canberra: Australian Government.

Australian Human Rights Commission (AHRC). (2009a). *Let's talk about rights: A guide to help young people have their say about human rights in Australia.* Sydney: Australian Human Rights Commission. Retrieved 9 March 2011 from: http://www.humanrights.gov.au/letstalkaboutrights/downloads/LTAR_youth_toolkit.pdf

Australian Human Rights Commission (AHRC). (2009b). *Submission to the National Human Rights Consultation.* June 2009. Retrieved 22 February 2010 from: http://www.humanrights.gov.au/legal/submissions/2009/nhrc/app6.html

Banaji, Shakuntala. (2008). 'The trouble with civic: a snapshot of young people's civic and political engagements in twenty-first-century democracies'. *Journal of Youth Studies, 11*(5), 543–60.

Batrouney, T. (2002). From 'White Australia' to multiculturalism: Citizenship and identity. In G. Hage (Ed.), *Arab-Australians today: Citizenship and belonging.* Carlton, VIC: Melbourne University Press, pp. 37–62.

Bradford, C. (2007). Cross-generational negotiations: Asian Australian picture books. *Papers: Explorations into children's literature, 17*(2), pp. 36–42.

Campbell, T. (1983). *The Left and Rights: A conceptual analysis of the idea of socialist rights.* London: Routledge and Kegan Paul.

Castles, S. (1996). The racisms of globalisations. In E. Vasta & S. Castles (Eds.), *The teeth are smiling: The persistence of racism in multicultural Australia* (pp. 17–45). St Leonards, NSW: Allen & Unwin.

Centenary of Federation Advisory Committee. (1994). 2001, *A report from Australia: A report to the Council of Australian Governments.* Canberra: Australian Government Publishing Service.

Civics Expert Group (CEG). (1994). *Whereas the people ... Civics and citizenship education.* Report of the Civics Expert Group. Canberra: Australian Government Publishing Service.

Cox, D. (1996). *Understanding Australia settlement services.* Canberra: Australian Government Publishing Service.

Curriculum Corporation. (2009). *Civics and citizenship education.* Retrieved 20 February 2010 from: http://www.civicsandcitizenship.edu.au/cce/background,8985.html

Davidson, A. (1997). *From subject to citizen: Australian citizenship in the twentieth century.* Cambridge: Cambridge University Press.

Delanty, G. (2000). *Citizenship in a global age: Society, culture, politics.* Buckingham: Open University Press.

Department of Immigration & Citizenship (DIC). (2009). *A new agenda for multicultural Australia.* Retrieved 21 February 2010 from: http://www.immi.gov.au/media/publications/multicultural/agenda/agenda1.htm

Forrest, J. (2009). *Report on attitudes towards and experience of racism among 18–24-year-olds in New South Wales, Queensland, Victoria and South Australia.* Melbourne: The Foundation for Young Australians.

Foster, S., Delaney, B., Bateman, A. & Dyson , C. (2007). *Higher-level vocational education and training qualifications: Their importance in today's training market.* Adelaide: NCVER.

Francis, S. & Cornfoot, S. (2007). *Multicultural youth in Australia: Settlement and transition.* Report for Australian Research Alliance for Children and Youth. Melbourne: Centre for Multicultural Youth Issues.

Galbally, F. (Chair) (1978). *Review of post-arrival program and services for migrants, migrant services and programs.* Canberra: Australian Government Publishing Service.

Hattam, R. (1995). Auditing democracy in the arena of teachers' work. *Flinders Institute for the Study of Teaching Newsletter,* No. 1, 1–4.

Hillier L., Turner A. & Mitchell, A. (2005). *Writing themselves in again – 6 years on: The second national report on the sexuality, health and wellbeing of same sex attracted young people.* Melbourne: Australian Research Centre in Sex Health and Society, La Trobe University.

House of Representatives Standing Committee on Education and Training (Commonwealth). (2009). *Adolescent overload? Report of the inquiry into combining school and work: Supporting successful youth transitions.* Canberra: Commonwealth of Australia.

House of Representatives Standing Committee on Legal and Constitutional Affairs (Commonwealth). (2009). *A time for change: Yes/No? Inquiry into the machinery of referendums.* Canberra: Commonwealth of Australia.

Howard, J. (2009). '2009 Menzies Lecture by John Howard'. *The Australian.* 22 August 2009. Retrieved 22 February 2010 from: http://www.theaustralian.com.au/politics/menzies-lecture-by-john-howard-full-text/story-e6frgczf-1225766613925

Joint Standing Committee on Electoral Matters. (2006). *Inquiry into Civics and Electoral Education.* Parliament of Australia. Retrieved 20 February 2010 from: http://www.aph.gov.au/house/committee/em/education/tor.htm

Joint Standing Committee on Migration. (1994). *Australians all — Enhancing Australian citizenship.* September 1994. Canberra: Australian Government Publishing Service.

Kukathas, C., Lovell, D. W., & Maley, W. (1990). *The theory of politics: An Australian perspective*. Melbourne: Longman Cheshire.

Lamb, S., & Mason, K. (2008). *How Young People are Faring 2008*. Melbourne: The Foundation for Young Australians.

Lamb, S., Robinson, L., & Walstab, A. (2010). *How Young People are Faring 2010*. Melbourne: The Foundation for Young Australians.

Lock, J., & Steiner, H. (1999). 'Gay, lesbian, and bisexual youth risks for emotional, physical, and social problems: Results from a community-based survey'. *Journal of the American Academy of Child and Adolescent Psychiatry, 38*, 297–304.

Long, M. & North, S. (2009). *How young Indigenous people are faring: Key indicators 1996– 2006*. Canberra: Dusseldorp Skills Forum

Mackay, H. (1993). *Reinventing Australia*. Sydney: Angus and Robertson.

Mansouri, F., Jenkins, L., Morgan, L., & Taouk, M. (2009). *The impact of racism upon the health and wellbeing of young Australians*. Melbourne: The Foundation for Young Australians.

Marshall, T. H. (1964). *Class, citizenship and social development*. New York: Doubleday.

Miller, T. (2001). Introducing … cultural citizenship. *Social Text, 69*, 19(4), 1–5.

Ministerial Council on Education, Employment, Training and Youth Affairs (MCEETYA). (2008). *Melbourne Declaration on Educational Goals for Young Australians*. Retrieved 31 March 2011 from: http://www.mceecdya.edu.au/mceecdya/default.asp?id=25979

Muir, K., Mullan, K., Powell, A., Flaxman, S., Thompson, D., & Griffiths, M. (2009). *State of Australia's young people: A report on the social, economic, health and family lives of young people*. NSW: Social Policy Research Centre, University of New South Wales.

National Multicultural Advisory Council. (1995). *Multicultural Australia: The next steps*. Canberra: Australian Government Publishing Service.

Office of Multicultural Affairs, Department of the Prime Minister and Cabinet. (1989). *National agenda for a multicultural Australia*. Canberra: Australian Government Publishing Service.

Ommundsen, W., Leach, M., & Vandenberg, A. (Eds.). (2010). *Cultural citizenship and the challenges of globalisation*. Cresskill, New Jersey: Hampton Press.

Organisation for Economic Co-operation and Development. (2009). *Jobs for youth: Australia*. Paris: OECD.

Pocock, B., Skinner, N., & Pisaniello, S. (2010). *How much should we work: Working hours, working holidays and working life: the participation challenge. The Australian Work and Life Index 2010*. The Centre for Work + Life, University of South Australia.

Print, M. (1995). 'From civics deficit to critical mass: The new civics education'. Based upon a paper delivered to the international conference 'Citizenship Education: Canadian and International Dimensions', St Thomas University, New Brunswick.

Retrieved 10 April 2010 from: http://www.abc.net.au/civics/teach/articles/mprint/ mprint1.htm

Robinson, L., & Lamb, S. (2009). *How Young People are Faring 2009*. Melbourne: The Foundation for Young Australians.

Salvaris, M. (1995). *Discussion Paper on a System of National Citizenship Indicators*. Canberra: Senate Legal and Constitutional References Committee.

Senate Standing Committee on Employment, Education and Training (SSCEET). (1989). *Education for active citizenship in Australian schools and youth organisations*. Canberra: Australian Government Publishing Service.

Stevenson, N. (2003). *Cultural citizenship: Cosmopolitan questions*. Maidenhead: Open University Press.

Victorian Health Promotion Foundation (VicHealth). (2009). *Building on our strengths: A framework to reduce race-based discrimination and support diversity in Victoria*. Melbourne: VicHealth.

Walsh, L. (2010). Six challenges to the social inclusion of young people in times of economic uncertainty. *Developing Practice: The Child, Youth and Family Work Journal, 26*, Spring, 21–29.

Walsh, L., & Leach, M. (2007). Recognising diversity: The challenges of multicultural education. In J. Connolly, M. Leach & L. Walsh (Eds.), *Recognition in politics: Theory, policy and practice* (pp. 115–27). Newcastle-upon-Tyne: Cambridge Scholars Publishing,

Warnock, B. (2008). 'Lower the voting age!' [*ActNow* website]. 26 June 2008. Retrieved 26 February 2010 from: http://www.actnow.com.au/Opinion/Lower_the_voting_ age.aspx

World Values Survey Association (www.worldvaluessurvey.org). (2009). *World Values Survey 2005* Official Data File v.20090901, 2009. Retrieved 2010 from: http://www. wvsevsdb.com/wvs/WVSData.jsp.

Wyn, J. (2010, April). *The making of a generation: Tracing the impact of social policies on Generation X*. Presentation to Forum on Research into 0–18 Learning and Development. Department of Education and Early Childhood Development, 23 April 2010. Retrieved 22 October 2010 from: http://www.eduweb.vic.gov.au/ edulibrary/public/publ/research/publ/0-18_presentation-johanna_wyn.pdf

Learning to participate

CHAPTER   2

Viewpoint 2:

Student participation – a personal perspective on the history and future of a really good idea

Johanna Wyn

My reflection starts out with the observation that for the last 30 years the same groups of children and young people have been identified as having poor educational outcomes: young people who are Indigenous; those from rural backgrounds and young people from low socio-economic communities. Over that time educationalists have become better at measuring the gaps between those who are successful in our education system and those who are failing. Experts are more effective at identifying the range of deficits in particular populations and can track the ways in which social and economic disadvantage is compounded through poor educational outcomes. My problem is that there is little evidence that identification of these measures has made a positive difference and many believe that it may have made things worse.

There is an emerging view that new approaches are needed to shift longstanding patterns of unequal outcomes. Another way of looking at this issue is to recognise that schools work best for groups whose cultural and social traditions align with school culture, and they work badly for those whose cultural and social experience diverge from traditional school cultures. In other words, schools are not neutral spaces – they are cultural and political organisations. This is pointed out by Richard Teese (2000) in his book *Academic Success and Social Power* where he shows how Australian schooling systems became polarised, with the most economically vulnerable populations of young people being the most likely to fail. He identifies the curriculum as a cultural and political tool that created disparities between groups of students. Schools as cultural sites are also analysed by Julie McLeod and Lyn Yates (2006) in their book *Making Modern Lives*. These authors point to the gaps and alignments between the social contexts of students and those of their teachers and schools as expressed in the school curriculum. Some young people manage to bridge the gap themselves but many do not. The effect of this is reflected in the chronic patterns of early school leaving in Australia.

Today, our research at the Youth Research Centre suggests the overwhelming majority of young people want to get a good education and understand that this is a key to achieving their employment and life goals. Despite this, too many young people continue to be disengaged from education.

A view from the 1980s

My engagement with this paradox began in the early 1980s, when I worked with a team of researchers at the Melbourne College of Advanced Education[1] on a program of research focusing on young people and their experiences of education and work. This program was the precursor to the Youth Research Centre at the University of Melbourne. The findings of the research program were published in the book *Shaping Futures* (Wilson & Wyn, 1987). The book makes a case for taking the priorities and contexts of young people, especially those in poor neighbourhoods, seriously. It argues that learning conditions are optimal when the curriculum actively forms a bridge between the perspectives and priorities of young people and their parents and those of educators. One of the case study schools was Fitzroy High School during the years 1982 to 1984, when the school served a largely working-class community of migrants from Greece and Italy who worked in the neighbouring factories. The parents wanted a better life for their children. The young people wanted to be involved in learning that would enable them to get good jobs – better and safer jobs than their parents were doing in the factories in the industrial estates that existed in Fitzroy and the neighbouring suburbs in the 1980s.

The book documents the lives of young people who attended Fitzroy Secondary School and two other schools in working-class suburbs of Melbourne as they negotiated their way through Year 10. Most of the students in the study followed the usual pattern of that time and left school before completing Year 12. The book explores the paradox that this occurred, despite the fact that these young people and their parents understood that education was a key to making a better life. The book

---

1   This team included Bruce Wilson, Peter Dwyer and Roger Woock.

concludes that although a profound mismatch was occurring, this was not a mismatch between the *goals* of the educators, parents and children. On the contrary, these three groups were in agreement about the preferred outcomes of education: better life chances for students and secure jobs. The mismatch occurred in the *practices* of educators in classrooms and in the school environment.

Shaping Futures concluded that for the common goals for educational success, held by parents, young people and educators, to be met, there needed to be a profound shift in the pedagogy. It argued for four principles that would provide a guide for the development of curricula that would address the needs of students in low socio-economic communities. It is in these communities that the cultural gap between curricula and students is the greatest. The four principles are:

- **The experience and concerns of students.** The social, political and economic context in which students are living tends to be seen almost entirely as a factor that impacts negatively on students' learning. Positive aspects of students' experiences can provide a powerful tool for developing curricula that engage them. The book identified a number of studies that show the extent to which students respond positively to school when their interests, concerns and circumstances are acknowledged in the curriculum.
- **The context of experience.** Because personal experience can also be limiting and possibly disempowering, a key role of school curricula is to examine the historical, social, economic and environmental context that has shaped young people's circumstances, locally and globally. This enables young people to see the connections between their current life circumstances and wider social and economic processes, and to understand what needs to be done to make change.
- **Integrated studies.** While academic disciplines remain a core element of school knowledge, integrated studies that draw across disciplines enable teachers and students to work with complex ideas in more applied ways. It is a more appropriate approach for developing an understanding of the complexity and dynamic of our rapidly changing society.
- **Negotiated learning processes.** This principle drew on the emerging interest in involving students in decision-making in schools and classrooms. It drew on evidence that when students can share resources and knowledge with each other they learn better and noted that negotiated learning equips young people to be lifelong learners.

These ideas were based on work with schools and communities undertaken 30 years ago. At that time, as now, young people from low socio-economic communities were the least likely of all groups to complete their secondary education. The four principles identified above aimed to provide principles for school curricula that would increase educational participation rates. They form four key elements of what we now call 'student participation'.

What has happened to student participation?

It would be tempting to conclude that during the 30 years that have elapsed since I and my colleagues wrote about the experiences of young people at Fitzroy Secondary School, student participation has failed to gain traction in Australian education. At a glance, this might appear to be the case. There are some striking examples that suggest young people are still not taken seriously and do not have opportunities to participate meaningfully in decisions about their education. A recent example is the 'My School' web site. Despite the claim made by its name, this site is not for young people. The information on levels of literacy and numeracy is intended for parents. The web site provides parents with the information they need to become more effective consumers of education. It will enable Australian educational markets to operate more effectively. The information serves the same purpose as the labelling on food products for sale on the supermarket shelves – it provides choice by enabling the consumer to decide what product offers the best price and value for them. In both cases, 'market forces' influence the kinds of products that are on offer. It begs the question of who schools are for and what a real 'My School' web site would look like – designed by and for students.

There are other examples that suggest student participation is not central to education today. For example, in 2010 a new national school curriculum was designed without consultation with or participation by young people. This is potentially one of the most significant contributions that the Rudd and Gillard governments will make to education. It aims to make Australian education 'world class'. Despite the statement in the *Melbourne Declaration* of 2008 that young Australians should be active and involved citizens, and that they should have responsibility for their education, young people's engagement with and participation in the development of the national curriculum was conspicuous by its absence.

Student participation is alive and well

It would however be simplistic to conclude that student participation is not practised in Australian schools, or that it is marginal. To the contrary, there is widespread recognition in schools and classrooms that effective learning involves a partnership between teachers and students (and communities). Indeed, as the newsletter *Connect* continues to demonstrate, student participation projects, programs, initiatives and practices have been a central component in many Australian schools for over 20 years.[2] I would draw attention to three strands of practice that are current in schools today.

Student participation as curriculum

Student Action Teams, introduced in Victoria in 1999, are an established approach within many Australian primary and secondary schools. This approach is based on the following principles: students are capable of making serious and important decisions about the issues that are important to them; students can do important and valuable things – they have skills, expertise and a knowledge of the needs of their community, and important action can be undertaken as part of students' learning in school; and community-focused research and action is an appropriate educational practice for schools to adopt.

In a Student Action Team, a group of students identify and tackle a school or community issue: they research the issue, make plans and proposals about it and take action on it, drawing on different subject areas such as mathematics, English, health and physical education, or history. Such initiatives, as part of the formal or informal school curriculum, engage students in purposeful, authentic activities which are valued by the students, which have broader community value and which meet or exceed mandated curriculum goals. Examples include doing research on bullying at school and making recommendations to the school council for action, surveying local traffic flows to petition the local council for safer traffic conditions around the school, and improving the safety and amenity of walkways between the railway station and the school. The three key elements that students gain

---

2   See *Connect*: <http://www.edfac.unimelb.edu.au/yrc/publications/connect.html>

from participating in their learning through Student Action Teams are: having a sense of purpose, having a sense of control, and gaining a sense of belonging. These outcomes continue to provide a compelling reason for teachers to practise student participation.

Student participation as classroom practice

Interactive learning tools can also promote participatory practices by positioning students and teachers as co-learners.[3] Dramaturgical interactive approaches provide structured processes through which young people are able to develop problem-solving skills about issues that are relevant to their lives and in which they have a strong participatory role. This approach has particular relevance in the health curriculum in relation to harm minimisation practices (e.g. in relation to alcohol or drugs) but it can also be used to explore values and relationships (e.g. in relation to bullying or diversity). It can also be used to develop inclusive practices that open up structured spaces in which young people and adults can communicate about learning. This use of dramaturgical practices challenges the traditional view of learning as teacher-dominated because it establishes ways of working that enable teachers to be open to learning from their students – and for students to learn from each other. It also challenges traditional views of curriculum by creating a space where students become partners in shaping what and how they learn. One of the strengths of this approach is that it enables curricula to be shaped around the issues that matter to young people and have meaning to them.

Student participation as a whole of school approach

Student participation is also central to the critically engaged learning approach. This approach is practised in a number of ways, including that espoused by Professor John Smyth and colleagues. They argue that educational participation is optimal when teachers 'recognise' the learners in their classroom. This means acknowledging where students come from –

---

3   I am indebted to Dr Helen Cahill at the Youth Research Centre for her work on dramaturgical pedagogies.

their history and that of their community. Many Indigenous educators also emphasise this approach to engaging young people in learning. This approach makes explicit patterns of disadvantage, social exclusion and marginalisation and operates from a social justice standpoint. It involves two key elements: the explicit acknowledgement of the role of education in communities and in community renewal, and giving parents and students greater control over learning in order to make it more meaningful. It is an approach that focuses on the assets that communities possess rather than focusing on deficits. It recognises the challenge of opening up educational and employment opportunities in communities where many people are living in poverty.

These three examples exemplify how the four principles described earlier are integral to initiatives that involve student participation. Each example takes students and their social context seriously, using students' experiences as a starting point. They emphasise the relevance of an integrated approach across curriculum areas and offer opportunities for students and teachers to negotiate the learning process, demonstrating the ongoing relevance of these basic principles.

Concluding comments

In 2009 I had the opportunity to revisit the question of young people's engagement with education through an invitation to author an Australian Education Review titled *Touching the Future: Building skills for life and work* (Wyn, 2009). This review of current thinking about the goals of Australian education identified the historic separation between the two main goals of education: i) the alignment of education with Australia's economic needs and ii) the promotion of an inclusive and democratic society. Although the first goal has dominated educational policy since the 1980s, the second goal has continued to exert a strong influence on the nature of school curricula. The Review concludes that both elements are necessary and desirable and argues that the challenge for educational practitioners and policy-makers is to design an expanded vision for Australian education that admits both of these goals equally.

Student participation is a really good idea because it provides a well-articulated framework for bridging these two essential goals of Australian education. There is now a strong evidence base that student participation works (see <www.fya.org.au/what-we-do/research/what-works/>).

There are other compelling reasons for taking student participation (and students) seriously.

1. Participatory approaches enable the teachers to design pedagogies (drawing on a national curriculum) to fit the circumstances of young people who are disengaged from or failing school. Connecting with local circumstances and conditions does not mean 'dumbing down' the curriculum. On the contrary, it may mean creating a more complex and critical curriculum that enables students to understand local and global processes that impact on their community. In this way, student participation enables these young people to have an experience of education that is more like their peers in more privileged areas, or who are more integrated into school culture: one in which they have a sense of purpose, a sense of control and of belonging.

2. Participatory approaches provide a framework within which Australian schools can acknowledge the increasingly diverse nature of the student population. The extent and nature of diversity is expanding across many dimensions, including the recognition of the needs of students with learning and physical disabilities, the increase in mental health problems, the increase in students who are refugees and the cultural diversity of students who are migrants. Participatory approaches offer a mechanism through which schools can identify the nature of their student population as a basis for establishing meaningful curricula.

3. Student participation recognises the changing role of 'the student'. The increase in older students attending school through improvements in retention rates as well as the impact of social change means that the boundaries between student and worker, child and adult, are also increasingly blurred. Schools that operate on student participation principles are more likely to provide an environment where these realities are recognised because the question of 'who is the learner' comes to the fore.

4. Poor relationships with teachers are the most frequent reason for students' disengagement from school. Participatory practices that position both teachers and students as partners in learning provide a process for creating relationships based on a better understanding of each other.

Addressing the longstanding problem of entrenched patterns of educational disadvantage requires conscious strategies and thoughtful educational designs. Relying on market forces to bring about educational change through patterns of educational consumption by discerning parents is a woefully inadequate way to create improved educational outcomes – education is too important to be left to market forces. The costs to both individuals and society of the current patterns of educational failure, low rates of attainment and alienation are too great to ignore.

This publication makes a timely intervention into the debate about how to move forward. The evidence suggests that a national curriculum that will lift educational standards for Australians and build the skills and knowledge that are needed for the 21st century will be based on student participation principles in its further development and implementation. This will ensure that curricula connect to the lives of all Australians, will enable them to see the relevance of what they are learning and to have control over their learning, and to experience schools as places where young people belong.

References

McLeod, J., & Yates, L. (2006). *Making modern lives: Subjectivity, schooling and social change.* Albany, NY: State University of New York Press.

Teese, R. (2000). *Academic success and social power: Examinations and inequality.* Carlton, VIC: Melbourne University Press.

Wilson, B., & Wyn, J. (1987). *Shaping futures: Youth action for livelihood.* Sydney, NSW: Allen & Unwin.

Wyn, J. (2009). Touching the future: Building skills for life and work. *Australian Education Review, 55.* Melbourne: Australian Council for Educational Research.

Johanna Wyn is a professor of education in the Melbourne Graduate School of Education and director of the Youth Research Centre at the University of Melbourne.

Case study 2:

ruMAD?

The ruMAD? (are you Making a Difference?) program provides a framework for young people's voice and action. Administered by FYA's Education Foundation division, it was developed by philanthropist Claire Brunner with consultant and former school principal, David Zyngier, and received its initial funding from the Stegley Foundation. Originally administered by Education Foundation, it is now managed by FYA. ruMAD? has been adopted by numerous schools, many of them serving disadvantaged communities. It has also been adopted by youth agencies, local government bodies and other non-educational organisations seeking to enable young people to enact social change within the community. This case study will focus on its use by schools.

The program's primary aim is to empower young people to take action in relation to issues that matter to them. It encourages young people to reflect on their values and priorities and to critically examine their role as active citizens. At the same time, its implementation within schools also serves to model independent, student-led learning for teachers. Independent evaluation shows that not all teachers are necessarily willing to adopt the principles upon which the program is based. It also shows that to be successful as a mechanism for youth participation, ruMAD? needs to unfold in a receptive environment where it is integrated into the culture of the school (Black et al., 2009; Stokes & Turnbull, 2008).

The eight keys of MADness

The ruMAD? program is structured using eight steps, and is divided into four phases.

1   Understanding phase

Values and vision

Here students are encouraged to talk openly about issues they are passionate about, and to share their stories and ideas in a confidential environment. Former program manager Josh Levy notes that the 'shift away from didactic learning helps to draw some students out'. The purpose of the session is to pinpoint issues or areas of interest that might form the basis for a social change project. Students are then helped to come to a democratic agreement about the issue they collectively choose to follow up.

MAD ideas

Students discuss what it means to make a difference in the world. As part of this, they compare stories of those they consider to be change-makers on a personal or a public level. Some students talk about celebrities, says Josh, 'but usually it's a discussion about my dad, or my footy coach, [people] who are obviously inspirational in some way and have made a difference to their life that's tangible and meaningful. So they can start to think "OK, that's how I'll know when I've achieved some kind of change"'.

Change not charity

A discussion forum introduces students to the notion of change rather than charity, and to the 'change metaphor': give a person a fish and they'll eat for a day; teach a person to fish and they'll eat for a lifetime; partner together and we can create our own sustainable fish supply. The central pedagogical message here is: tell me and I'll forget; show me and I'll remember; involve me and I'll understand.

Creating a project

Students use brainstorming techniques to come up with a formal project proposal. Teachers and ruMAD? facilitators do not guide or direct the nature of the project, but help students to break down broad concepts and focus their ideas. Josh explains: 'A lot of them say "poverty". OK great, what's that? That part of the inquiry process is then to go away and learn about poverty, and they'll come back and find that poverty is made up of lack of access to health care, lack of food, lack of shelter, whatever it might be'. The particular project devised by students often correlates with issues receiving attention in the media or current affairs or, naturally enough, with the local politics of the area in which they live. The nature of the project varies enormously: it might be a one-off event or the more ambitious creation of a student foundation or social enterprise.

2   Planning phase

Planning change

Having created a project proposal, students set to work planning its implementation. They must be sure the project is SMART: Specific, Measurable, Achievable, Realistic and Timely. The 'Time, Talent and Treasure' exercise encourages students to identify exactly what amounts of time and what specific skills and materials they can bring to the project.

Getting what you need

Students make connections with community organisations and individuals who can partner with them in their social change project, or provide them with valuable information. FYA has an important role here as a broker, connecting students with experts from groups like headspace, beyondblue, Urban Seed or The Big Issue.

3   Action phase

Creating change

In putting their project into action, students are encouraged to gather evidence around its effectiveness and check progress. Many projects have the potential to grow: 'Eighty per cent of these programs could become a social enterprise if that student was old enough to leave school ... the fact that they've created a project or initiative that has the potential to generate an income source but has a social cause at its root is a winner', says Josh.

4   Evaluation and celebration phase

Reflect and celebrate

The final stage of the ruMAD? program is a celebration of what has been achieved as a result of the students' work. Participants are encouraged to reflect on the process – positives and negatives – and to mark the occasion with something like a performance, a conference, a publication, an exhibition or a community event.

Melbourne Girls' College Student Foundation

While many ruMAD? initiatives take the form of specific, time-limited projects, the program also lends itself to more ambitious or sustainable youth participation initiatives. At Melbourne Girls' College, this has taken the form of a sustainable youth philanthropy initiative – the Student Foundation.

Melbourne Girls' College sits alongside the Yarra River in inner-urban Richmond. Its student population of around 1200 is extraordinarily diverse, with girls born in 60 different countries and living in over 200 Victorian postcodes. In 2001, the College established Australia's first student foundation through the ruMAD? program, with financial assistance from the Myer Foundation and the Council for the Encouragement of Philanthropy in Australia.

By brainstorming 'values and vision', as outlined in phase one of ruMAD?, the original student group settled on the core values of equality, compassion, trust, loyalty, truth, respect and honesty, community and family. Their areas of passion were identified as safety in the community, depression and suicide, homelessness and poverty, and equal rights. The foundation's mission statement was agreed upon as follows:

> We wish to further a society that values community and family based on compassion, trust, loyalty, truth, respect and honesty with equality of opportunity and rights for young women. We will do this through supporting projects that address youth alienation, community safety, social disadvantage and equality of opportunity.

The foundation works with limited funds, relying on two casual clothes days per year that draw a gold coin donation from students. It offers grants of up to $2000 and mini-grants of $500. Nia Holdenson, Director of Girls' Leadership, has overseen the operation of the foundation since its inception and notes that the greatest challenges faced by those involved lie in the engagement of other students, and the tax status of the foundation. Being attached to a government school, it was unable to join with other philanthropic organisations – like the Melbourne Community Foundation – and instead exists as 'a line of entry in the school books', says Nia. Donations are not tax-deductible and the foundation must rely on the generosity of students and parents over and above the cost of school fees, uniforms and extracurricular activities.

In its earliest stages, the foundation was run by the treasurer of the student executive by default. Since then, the creation of two official positions – Philanthropy Captain and Vice Captain – has increased the profile of the foundation within the school, but the concept of philanthropy remains unfamiliar for many. One student explains that 'being titled the Student Foundation, people think that the money is going into the school when in fact it's going out ... until you really get that across sometimes it's like drawing blood from a stone'.

The foundation's first grant went to the 'Cookin's Cool' project at the Brosnan Centre in Brunswick for young offenders recently released from prison or juvenile detention centres. The Centre used the grant of $1200 to buy a barbecue and invited students from Melbourne Girls' College to join the young men for lunch, encouraging social interaction. Nia explains:

> [The Brosnan Centre] felt that it was a boy's job cooking at a barbecue, you know how men stand at a barbecue and talk, and if the men learnt social skills then when they partnered they would be more likely to partner wisely and bring up better children. So even though we were working towards women in the community, by giving the grant to the men it was going to reflect back onto the women.

Some of the most successful projects came from mini-grants, particularly when local primary schools were invited to apply. The Student Foundation team was heavily involved in selecting applicants: 'We went to those schools and the schools told us about their idea, and the little panel of girls – as many as I could fit in my car which was four – asked them questions', says Nia. One of the schools, Lloyd Street Primary School, used the money to buy felt to make a wall hanging for the local elderly persons' home. Students from Richmond North Public School bought books to read to children at the local kindergarten.

Like all philanthropic endeavours, the foundation has funded a number of projects with less satisfactory results or encountered grant recipients who were unable to explain how money had been spent; but the primary aim is for the girls to understand the community responsibility that comes with economic independence. The key, says one student, is in giving to projects that resonate with the student body. A recent grant went to sponsor a female student to complete her Victorian Certificate of Education through a program in Vanuatu. The founder of the program visited Melbourne Girls' College to speak to the students, and the impact of the visit was immediate. Further funds have gone to a tutoring program for disadvantaged students established by a former school captain of the College. Asked about the future of the foundation, the school's Philanthropy Captain reflects:

> I'd like to see it flourishing. I'd like it to be known around the community and, if organisations are looking for help and others know our core values, that we can be recommended as a source. I'd like every girl in the school to know what the Student Foundation is and why we have it. And I think just for the foundation itself to receive recognition because I know it's an inanimate object with money going in and out, but the people it's helped and everything that it's done is such a step for philanthropy, particularly in schools. And I'd like to see other schools – not necessarily have the exact same thing – but develop their own, because each school is unique and, like I said, this is our first step. I think we've got many steps to go but we're definitely on the right track. I couldn't see it ending, I can't see that.

References

Black, R., Stokes, H., Turnbull, M., & Levy, J. (2009). 'Civic participation through the curriculum', *Youth Studies Australia, 28*(3), 13–20.

Stokes, H., & Turnbull, M. (2008). *Real engagement with real issues: An evaluation of the ruMAD? program*. Melbourne: Education Foundation

Interview with Joshua Levy (Barbara Lemon), 7 July 2009.

Interview with Nia Holdenson and Catherine Ross (Barbara Lemon and Melissa Ibrihim, Melbourne Girls' College), 3 August 2009.

Commentary 2:

Citizenship and participation in schools

Rosalyn Black

A mandate for participation?

This commentary relates the findings of my PhD study, which is being undertaken at time of writing with the Youth Research Centre at the University of Melbourne. The study investigates the capacity of schools in low socio-economic contexts to meet the policy expectation that they enable young people's democratic participation. This commentary outlines the need for such investigation and, in so doing, considers the forces that are shaping the way in which the citizenship and democratic participation of young Australians is understood and approached by a key social institution – the school.

Australian educational policy clearly expects that young people have an active role in the processes and structures of civic society. It also clearly expects that schools will be the primary locus for the development of young people's capacity and willingness to participate in these processes and structures. This reflects the longstanding recognition that schools are ideal institutions for transmitting social norms such as civic participation and for developing the skills and knowledge required to meet these norms. It also follows a longstanding policy tradition which frames schools as institutions that serve a set of agreed public purposes, including the development of young people's ability to participate as citizens.

As Lucas Walsh explains in Chapter 1, the trend is for policy initiatives designed to foster young people's participation to focus on a formal curriculum for civics and citizenship education. In Australia, the potential of the curriculum to foster young people's democratic competencies was identified by a series of Senate inquiries, committees and reports commissioned by the federal government during the late 1980s and 1990s. These culminated in a report by the Civics Expert Group that recommended the development of a national curriculum to improve the democratic literacy of young Australians (Civics Expert Group, 1994). With federal funding, a formal curriculum for citizenship education was introduced in 1997, first in the form of the Discovering Democracy curriculum, and later as the national Civics and Citizenship Education program.

A number of current policy documents describe the competencies that young people are expected to be able to acquire and demonstrate as a result of this curriculum. They make it clear what role Australian schools are expected to play in enabling young people to participate in society.

The Australian Government's *Statements of Learning for Civics and Citizenship*, for example, describe a set of skills and knowledge that include 'an understanding of, and commitment to, Australia's democratic system of government, law and civic life', 'the capacity to clarify and critically examine values and principles that underpin Australia's democracy and the ways in which these contribute to a fair and just society', 'the knowledge, skills and values that support active citizenship and the capacity to act as informed and responsible citizens' and 'an appreciation of the local, state, national, regional and global rights and responsibilities of citizenship and civic life' (Curriculum Corporation, 2006, p. 2). The *National Framework for Values Education in Australian Schools* articulates a vision for Australian schooling that includes the development of 'student responsibility in local, national and global contexts' (Department of Education, Science and Training, 2005, p. 3). Its Nine Values for Australian Schooling expect that young Australians will be equipped through their schooling to 'enjoy all the rights and privileges of Australian citizenship', 'pursue and protect the common good where all people are treated fairly for a just society' and 'contribute to society and to civic life' (2005, p. 4). As an adjunct to these national statements, the secondary school curriculum frameworks of all Australian states and territories now include a measurable expectation that young people will be equipped with the knowledge and skills for participation in democratic processes (Department of Immigration and Citizenship, 2009).

Beyond these curricular expectations, the *Melbourne Declaration on Educational Goals for Young Australians* provides Australian schools with a clear brief to foster young people's participation. The *Melbourne Declaration* is the most universal and highly authorised current policy statement for Australian schooling. Released in 2008 and endorsed by all state, territory and Commonwealth ministers of education through the then Ministerial Council on Education, Employment, Training and Youth Affairs (MCEETYA), it represents a blueprint for Australian schooling for the next decade. Its authority is bolstered by the accompanying MCEETYA Four Year Plan, which was endorsed by all ministers in 2009 and is aligned with the work of the Council of Australian Governments. Its second goal is to enable all young Australians to become 'active and informed citizens' who 'participate in Australia's civic life, ... work for the common good (and) are responsible global and local citizens' (MCEETYA, 2008, p. 8).

Like a lot of policy statements, the *Melbourne Declaration* and the other policy texts I have cited earlier have an innate confidence and authority. Their language is positive and optimistic. They are forward-looking and future-focused. They strongly imply and infer a stable and successful society to which, given the right educational opportunities, young people can readily contribute and belong. They provide a clear mandate to Australian schools to enable young people to develop the skills and dispositions for participation in society. What is considerably less clear is how schools are expected to enact this mandate or what forces may affect its enactment. What is absent from the policy texts is a recognition of the complexity that characterises the democratic participation of young people. They overlook the almost complete lack of consensus within schools about the form that young people's participation should take, the purposes it should serve and the outcomes it should deliver. They also overlook the prevailing culture and political nature of schooling and their effect on how – and indeed on whether – schools enact their mandate.

Commentators such as Nudzor have described the policy process as one that entails 'mixed feelings and values, pragmatism, micropolitics, frustration, and muddle' (2009, p. 502). This muddle is particularly apparent when it comes to young people's participation. If participation has become a policy '"buzz" term' (Hadfield & Haw, 2001, p. 485) or even 'a policy cliché' (Bessant 2004, p. 387), there is little agreement about what it actually denotes. Instead, it remains a sliding signifier that is subject to a range of interpretations and applications and serves a range of agendas (Apple, 2002). Commentators from the United States have noted that 'if educators can agree that schools have a role to play in educating democratic citizens, they can't seem to agree on what that means' (Westheimer & Kahne, 2003, p. 3). Similar observations have been made about Australia.

This lack of agreement is encapsulated in numerous typologies that demonstrate some of the ways in which young people's participation can be interpreted by schools. Thomson and Holdsworth, for example, describe a wide spectrum of student participation that ranges from 'being physically present at school' to 'community or social activism' (2003, pp. 373–374).

Mitra's pyramid of student voice ranges from 'being heard' to 'building capacity for leadership' (2006, p. 7). Holdsworth proposes a student participation ladder whose rungs range from 'speaking out' to 'sharing decision-making (and) implementation of action' (2000, p. 358). Fielding's typology ranges from students serving as a source of data for school processes to students acting as active researchers who drive change within the school (2001).

Worryingly, the evidence is that dominant practice in Australian schools clusters around the lowest rungs of these various ladders. Research commissioned by FYA shows that initiatives to support young people's participation are burgeoning across numerous non-educational contexts (Kimberley 2010; Taylor 2010a, 2010b), but schools appear to be lagging behind.

Participating in school governance

Schools present 'both opportunities and constraints' for young people's participation (Rasmussen & Harwood, 2009, p. 6). Sadly, it is the constraints that are usually the most in evidence.

Describing Australian schools more than a decade ago, Walsh and Salvaris concluded that 'schools are imperfect models for democracy' (1998, p. 28). Around the same time, Holdsworth noted that students are 'encouraged to have a "voice", but no more' (2000, p. 358), and Wilson concluded that student participation was not an 'entrenched characteristic' of Australian schools (2000, p. 31). Four years later, Johnson accused Australian schools of teaching about democracy 'within school contexts where undemocratic practices abound' (2004, p. 6). A further three years later, Print noted that little had changed (2007).

We are still waiting for signs that conditions will ever be different. Despite the growing policy emphasis on youth participation, young people remain routinely excluded from real participation in the operation or governance of their schools. This is not because they are complacent or uninterested in having such a role. Australian students, in particular, strongly believe that they could make a beneficial contribution to the operation of their schools but do not feel that their participation is well supported (Mellor & Kennedy, 2003). This is by contrast with some of their international counterparts, who seem unaware that the potential exists for their participation. A Canadian study, for example, found that even having a say in school decision-making was unimaginable for students, whose participation was described as ranging from 'dismal' to 'sparse' (Raby, 2008, p. 83). A New Zealand study produced parallel findings: of 66 students asked to describe how they might participate in their school, only one recognised that this could include participation in the school's decision-making processes (Taylor, Smith & Gollop, 2008).

The exclusion of young people from these processes persists despite the trend towards distributed school leadership, which aims to drive improvement by leveraging the contribution of all stakeholders within the school (Walsh & Black, 2009). Students are surely the most important stakeholders in any school, yet they remain the group that is least frequently invited to share in the governance or decision-making processes of their schools and whose role within these processes is most limited. It persists despite the trend towards new community-centred models of schooling designed to maximise the contribution of the school community to its governance and operating structures and engage the wider community in the work of schools (Black, 2008a, 2008b, 2009; Black & Walsh, 2009). Even within these emerging and more democratic models of schooling, the contribution of young people is frequently overlooked.

It is also overlooked despite the abundant evidence that the implementation of any curriculum for citizenship education without accompanying mechanisms for genuine participation has a marked impact on the efficacy of that curriculum. The most recent assessment of citizenship education in Australia shows that schools that provide greater opportunities for student participation show higher average achievement in the citizenship curriculum than other schools, and that individual students who participate to a greater degree achieve better than those who participate to a lesser degree (MCEETYA, 2009).

Even in cases where schools encourage their participation, limits are placed on the degree of influence young people are permitted to assume. Perhaps because of this, the most common vehicle for student participation in school governance remains the Student Representative Council (SRC) or its analogous structures.

While Australian teachers view the SRC as an important means of building students' capacity to participate in the life of the school (Mellor, Kennedy & Greenwood, 2001), many SRCs operate in a superficial way that is clearly not intended to have a significant impact on school processes. In fact, schools' persistent preference for channelling student participation through SRCs may indicate the attractiveness of what is both an adult model and one that can be constrained by adults. In many of its incarnations, the SRC is shaped by teachers, both in its organisation and conduct and in the issues that it addresses. This is in preference to structures that reflect the issues that young people care about and the way in which they may want to address these issues (Cairns, 2001). This adoption of an adult-centric model of youth participation is certainly not limited to schools, but its prevalence in schools does require critical assessment. If, as some commentators have suggested, schools are afraid of giving students a genuine role in their decision-making processes in case their perceptions and suggestions are too challenging to the status quo (Gunter & Thomson, 2007), it seems unlikely that the ambitious vision of the *Melbourne Declaration* will be realised at any time soon.

There are also concerns that SRCs provide opportunities for too few students: a research review supported by FYA has concluded that only four per cent of Australian secondary school students are members of their SRC (Collin, 2008). In particular, SRCs tend to engage those students who are already confident, articulate or recognised leaders, but overlook those who are not. These may include students whose voices are seen as marginal, such as those from lower socio-economic groups or those who do not conform to the normative behaviours of the classroom or the school. Smyth argues that 'schools are deeply implicated in drawing boundaries around those who are deemed to be successful learners and those who are not' (2006, p. 12). In too many instances, the same may be said for those who are permitted to participate.

This is certainly not to criticise or condemn the notion of a student council or representative body out of hand. The case study of ruMAD? at Melbourne Girls' College, for example, describes an innovative youth philanthropy initiative that emerged out of the student executive. Other examples of ruMAD? in action also utilise the SRC or its equivalent as a vibrant focal point for student voice and participation. The concern that comes out of the research literature is more that student participation is too readily contained and constrained. In worst cases, the vehicle identified as the main or even the only means by which young people can have influence within their school is seriously compromised, both in relation to the scope of influence it enables and the number and diversity of students it welcomes. This is particularly problematic in the face of the growing diversity of young people in Australian schools.

When it comes to the workings of educational systems beyond the governance of individual schools, young people are even more on the outer. Despite sophisticated arguments that students' particular knowledge and perspectives improve the efficacy of efforts to reform schooling, they are still typically perceived as the passive recipients or objects of educational reform. In 2002, Bentley suggested that 'young people themselves are probably the greatest untapped resource in the process of educational transformation' (p. 15). The evidence is that they are still an untapped resource.

Participating in the classroom

Giving students a role in school governance is only one way in which schools can engender young people's participation. Another and perhaps more important way for young people to participate is through the curriculum and pedagogy of the classroom. We already know that the climate of the classroom is pivotal in fostering the skills and dispositions for citizenship and participation. We also know that isolated student participation initiatives do not 'suddenly make schools into democracies' (Davies et al., 2009, p. 35). Instead, if schools are to become more democratic spaces, teachers need to adopt a more democratic approach within the classroom. It is not as though we lack blueprints for this democratic practice: numerous studies and initiatives have described and demonstrated what a genuinely democratic or participatory classroom could look like.

Over the past decade, Australian schools have had access to a rolling series of approaches that foster this kind of practice. These include inquiry-based and constructivist approaches characterised by high levels of student decision-making; authentic or productive pedagogies which emphasise the connectedness of the curriculum to students' lives; community-based learning that locates education in the environment in which students live; and negotiated learning, where the curriculum is planned collaboratively by teachers and students. In some instances, these student-centred approaches to teaching and learning have been adopted as significant reform strategies designed to change the culture of the school (Black, 2007).

These approaches are not only good educational practice: they also provide the kind of environment in which participation is most likely to flourish. This is an environment in which the content transmitted through the curriculum acknowledges and reflects students' experience, identities, values and concerns beyond the classroom walls. It is also an environment in which they are encouraged to explore and debate social and political issues and, potentially, to take action to address them. It is an environment in which students can engage in forms and arenas of participation that give them 'presence, power, and agency' (Cook-Sather, 2006, p. 363).

In practice, many classrooms fall short of this prescription. Instead, many young Australians feel that their schools are not interested in their views or experience (Harris, Wyn & Younes, 2008). They do not feel free to disagree with their teachers about social or political issues, to generate their own views of such issues or to state these views within the classroom (Mellor & Kennedy, 2003). This is in sharp contrast to their experience outside school, where many young people regularly communicate and debate their views with a wide online community. The case study of SYN (included in Chapter 3) is a strong reminder of the kind of communicative agency and autonomy that young people are regularly demonstrating in non-school settings. It stands in sharp contrast to the tacit assumption that operates in too many classrooms that young people's values and voices are somehow superfluous to their educational experience.

What makes things worse is that the constraints placed on young people's voices within the classroom are often invisible. Bragg has described an 'implicit contract' underpinning much of the practice of student participation in schools, whereby students are expected to participate 'responsibly, intelligibly and usefully' (2001, p. 70). Needless to say, the way in which responsibility and usefulness is constructed is not determined by the students themselves. Like so many other aspects of schooling, it is determined by the culture of the classroom and the school. Corbett and Wilson have described the way in which students comply with teacher expectations by 'attempt(ing) to construct the meanings they think the teacher expects them to derive from some activity' (1995, p. 13). What we may be seeing in many classrooms that purportedly support student participation is a surface or superficial appearance of participation that tells us nothing about whether young people value it as an important aspect of their identity. In an environment where participation becomes just another educational task or hurdle, young people may comply with its requirements without being either engaged or inspired.

Changing this picture may be a difficult process. One study notes that 'even in nations such as Australia, where changing youth civic identity and learning styles have been recognized, educational institutions often prove resistant to change' (Bennett, Wells & Rank, 2008, p. 5).

Teachers are frequently charged with leading this resistance and there is certainly evidence that not all teachers are on board. Some actively oppose the introduction of student participation practices because they are sceptical about its purposes or its relevance to the educational project, or because they are concerned about its potential to change the nature and dynamic of the classroom (Davies, 2009). Others adopt a stance of more passive resistance. In some cases, this may mean that they enact student participation practice because it is mandated by the school but remain unconvinced of its value. In other cases, it may mean that they agree with or subscribe to the principle of student participation as an abstract notion without enacting it in practical or effective ways within the classroom (Cleaver et al., 2005).

As a collective, however, Australian school teachers have a long history of commitment to notions of equity and student empowerment. Many – myself included – have cut their professional teeth on the writings of such educationalists as Connell, Smyth and Thomson, to mention just a few, whose work argues passionately for an inclusive and democratic educational system. The suggestion that teachers are blocking the road to young people's participation requires further investigation in the light of this history. Teacher ambivalence about student voice in the classroom can be based on real and valid concerns about their professional identity and purpose. For many teachers, the adoption of new pedagogical practice can be seriously challenging (Black, 2007). An increased adoption of practice that gives young people a new role in the classroom and a new voice within the school can also require the creation of a new pedagogical identity for the teacher. On top of the considerable pressures that come with the acquisition of new practice, then, teachers may also feel that their previous or existing practice has been rendered unsatisfactory or incomplete (Bragg, 2007). This cannot be treated lightly: if schools are to become places that foster real student participation, teachers have to have the professional training and support they need to make this happen.

The suggestion that teachers are standing in the way of greater student participation also requires further investigation in the light of conflicting observations about the degree to which they actually determine the culture, practice and policy of the school. Where teachers are frequently seen as 'the gatekeepers of change' (Rudduck & Demetriou, 2003, p. 280), it may be that, particularly within the current culture of schooling, many have less autonomy than this suggests. This lack of autonomy can be seen at the level of the school, where tensions may arise if teachers attempt to instigate participatory practices without the support of school leadership (Thomson, 2002). It can also be seen at the level of the system. In an environment of rising policy prescriptiveness, teachers may find little room for their democratic values and practices (Taylor & Robinson, 2009). This issue will be considered in greater depth later in this commentary.

Participation for whom?

The resurgence of policy interest in young people's participation also has another and, perhaps, a darker side. Internationally, this policy interest has been accompanied from the start by a view that young people lack civic and political knowledge and make less contribution to society than older people. This view has not arisen by itself: it is reinforced by numerous studies including a recent study for the Australian Government (Muir et al., 2009). The risk is that instead of recognising the numerous ways in which young people are already participating, the policy of 'participation' may reinforce what is already a persistent deficit discourse about young people.

Schooling already generates its own deficit discourse about young people. While Australia is not alone in this regard, the culture of Australian schooling has been accused of failing to recognise the changing nature of youth and young people's experience. This shows itself in the way in which many schools remain strongly influenced by a developmental conceptualisation of youth, which sees it as a transitional stage on the way to adulthood rather than a period in which young people are already active agents within their own lives. Growing concerns about the safety and wellbeing of young people and the litigious environment that has sprung up around these concerns have only added to an environment in which schools increasingly act as 'caretakers' of young people (Raby, 2008, p. 78). As Johanna Wyn has pointed out, this infantilisation of young people sits oddly with their experience outside the school, where a growing number are engaged in part-time work that requires and assumes high levels of responsibility and autonomy (Wyn, 2009). It also sits uncomfortably with their experiences at home, where decisions that affect young people are frequently made jointly with their parents (Danby & Farrell, 2004).

This points to a recurrent tension within the policy literature between a discourse that emphasises young people's agency as members of society and a discourse that strongly infers their developmental status as 'adults in waiting'. This tension is evident within key documents such as the *National Framework for Values Education in Australian Schools*, which describes young people's 'potential life roles as family, community and workforce members' and makes it clear that these roles will only commence for young people 'when they leave school' (Department of Education, Science and Training, 2005, p. 2). The further implication of such statements is that democratic participation is conditional on the acquisition of a specific set of skills and capacities and that, simply because they are young, young people lack these skills and capacities.

While young people are expected to develop the behaviours and knowledge on which civic society relies, therefore, they are rarely positioned as integral current members of this society. Instead, they are consistently treated as though they stood 'outside the full umbrella of citizenship' (Raby, 2008, p. 78). This is particularly evident in the inference that schooling should prepare young people for their role as citizens. While this sort of statement has become ubiquitous within educational policy to the point of cliché, like all clichés it warrants a deeper scrutiny. Its clear meaning is that participation is a future state or status that young people can only attain through the educational experience.

This creates a normative construction of young people's citizenship that is inherently exclusive. It excludes young people from their current and present rights and responsibilities as members of society because it defers these rights and responsibilities until some future time, namely the time when they complete their school education. It excludes them from any current membership as citizens because it overlooks any existing forms of participation or social action in which they may already be engaged: the educational interventions inspired by this discourse, such as citizenship education, are based on a presumption that their purpose is to enable young people to make the transition from a 'predemocratic' state into a state where they qualify for democratic participation (Biesta, 2010, p. 124). Perhaps most insidiously, it also excludes young people who may not succeed or stay at school. If schooling is the vehicle by which young people are to obtain the means and capacities for recognised social participation, what does this mean for young people who are disengaged from school, who leave school early or who do not succeed educationally? The inference is that they will be permanently locked out of the social compact.

Instead of offering expanded opportunities, therefore, the strong policy link between schooling and participation may in fact reinforce the marginalisation to which young people are routinely subject.

As I have implied, the greatest burden of these deficit discourses falls on those young people who are already marginalised. In particular, young people from low socio-economic backgrounds suffer from a deficit of opportunities to participate. They typically demonstrate less civic knowledge than their more affluent peers (Torney-Purta et al., 2001) and are less likely to achieve well in civics and citizenship studies (MCEETYA, 2009). They are less likely to volunteer (Lerner, Alberts & Bobek, 2007), less likely to have the opportunity to belong to youth organisations that provide the experience of participation (Watts & Flanagan, 2007), less likely to have faith in civic and political institutions (Anderton & Abbott, 2009), less likely to engage in the behaviours that facilitate participation (Brown, Lipsig-Mumme & Zajdow, 2003) and less likely to participate in their community (Spring, Dietz & Grimm, 2007). They are less likely to have a strong sense of agency and control over their own lives or to believe that their actions can make a difference (Benton et al., 2008) and more likely to be excluded from opportunities to make key decisions in relation to their lives (Wierenga, 2003). They are also less likely to have access to the kind of learning opportunities through their schools that would promote their participation (Kahne & Middaugh, 2008). This last point is perhaps the most worrying of all, because of its implication that young people from disadvantaged backgrounds are not being given access to the kind of quality learning environment which I described earlier and which has been widely accepted as the educational right and entitlement of all young people.

Despite this compelling evidence that change is needed and despite the encouraging signals from the *Melbourne Declaration* in particular, educational policy continues to overlook the issue of equity in determining which young people participate. This may be partly a product of the way in which policy – including educational policy – increasingly conflates all young people as a single group or subset of society, assuming and transmitting a homogenised and normative conception of youth that 'obscure[s] the significance of increasing inequalities and differences between groups of young people' (Wyn & Woodman, 2006, p. 511). This homogenised view persists despite the strong Australian policy focus on social inclusion. It also persists despite the clear evidence that inequity continues to be one of the strongest features of the Australian schooling landscape (Keating, 2009, 2010).

Participation for what?

I began this commentary with a brief description of some of the signals that indicate an increasing popularity of the notion of youth or student participation within Australian educational environments. At first glance, this popularity would appear to be an entirely positive development. Looking deeper, however, there are a number of barriers to the realisation of its full potential. As I have already explained, some of these barriers are located at the level of the classroom or the school. Others are located at the level of educational systems.

The greatest systemic barrier to the capacity of schools to better recognise and support young people's democratic participation may be the plethora of other demands and expectations being placed on them by systems and jurisdictions. In an era where schools are under increased pressure to meet a host of policy and bureaucratic requirements, there is a danger that they adopt or enact student participation initiatives simply to comply with policy expectations. Even schools that have a demonstrated commitment to young people's participation are challenged by the need to navigate competing agendas and accountabilities. In schools with a lesser level of commitment or with higher levels of pressure to demonstrate their performance against state and national targets, student participation can readily degenerate into another means of increasing young people's attendance, engagement and compliant behaviour (Thornberg, 2009).

This is not to overlook the importance of educational engagement or the potential role of student participation in improving it (Black et al., 2009). However, initiatives motivated solely by student engagement may be more motivated by system targets than by a genuine belief in the value of young people's role in society. In this case, they are likely to reinforce and propagate forms of student participation that are superficial and tokenistic. One risk of this situation is its impact on young people, who are likely to become cynical about democratic processes and structures if the promise of participation does not translate into the kind of agency they expect to experience or into the kind of impact they wish to see (Whitty & Wisby, 2007).

Another risk is that the current policy interest in young people's participation and citizenship may simply 'burn out before its transformative potential has been fully understood' (Rudduck & Demetriou, 2003, p. 285). The evidence is that we are headed in this direction. Australian schooling policy, like that of other OECD nations, is characterised by an increasing emphasis on standards, performance and accountability. This is creating a hardened policy climate (Angus, 2006) which has been linked to a 'dedemocratization' of schools and schooling (Apple, 2004, p. 618), and which has numerous implications for schools' capacity to foster and encourage the kind of agentic participation that young people want and deserve.

This is partly because a more centralised educational policy environment has a constraining effect on the school's ability to provide the sort of curriculum and pedagogy that is conducive to young people's social participation. It also has a constraining effect on the school's ability to reflect the value of that participation through measurement and assessment. The emerging findings of one study in which FYA is involved shows that the work of schools is highly subject to external forces in the form of funding and bureaucratic constraints (Reid et al., 2010).

It is also partly because an educational policy environment that is gravitating towards more rigid or closed measurements of educational success leaves little room for the more transformative interpretations of young people's participation. These transformative interpretations link active citizenship and social participation to deep notions of democracy. They position them as the key to the creation of a genuinely inclusive society that is characterised by equity and justice and that has the internal will and capacity to critically assess, challenge and change those of its structures that impede equity and justice. They imagine a role for young people in the vanguard of such a society, acting as autonomous social agents with the capacity for 'civic courage' (Giroux, 1990, p. 194).

These social visions are certainly not absent from the policy context. The *Melbourne Declaration*, for example, proposes that 'a school's legacy to young people should include national values of democracy, equity and justice' (MCEETYA, 2008, p. 5). There is no doubt that these values are highly attractive. Few of us would argue with the proposition that they should be guiding principles for both the current and future state of Australian society. Few of us would debate the proposal that young people should contribute to such an agenda. What is hidden in this picture is something more fundamental, so fundamental that it is often overlooked: it is the fact that these values are prescribed for and on behalf of young people. They are presented as a set of pre-existing national values to which young people are expected to adhere and which they are expected to uphold and perpetuate. The implication is that the behaviour we seek from young people as citizens is to subscribe to an *existing* vision, however attractive it may be, but not to have a role in deciding or determining that vision. The dominant message emerging from even the most visionary policy literature still runs counter, therefore, to the notion that young people are and should be recognised as autonomous social agents and actors.

Conclusion

If we accept that 'education policy is democratic inasmuch as it supports equality of opportunity and outcome for all students and promotes social mobility rather than reproduction' (Perry, 2009, p. 436), it may be that education policy in countries such as Australia is embracing democratic purposes in theory without serving them in practice. This is not helped by persistent gaps in our research and knowledge.

We still do not know enough about the capacity of schools, especially schools in low socio-economic and high-need contexts, to meet the policy expectation that they enable young people's participation. We don't know enough about the degree to which teachers feel sufficiently informed, supported and authorised to put this policy expectation into action. We don't know enough about how the enactment of student participation is understood and experienced by the young people at whom it is directed. We don't know enough about what young people want and expect in regards to their participation in and through their schools.

We do know that many young people are well aware of the way in which they are almost ritually marginalised and excluded through their schooling experience. We know that they are keenly aware that they sit 'at the bottom of the education status list' (Levin, 2000, p. 155). We also know that they are frustrated by the hypocrisy of a schooling system that overlooks their present capacities but expects them to 'take the reins of a democratic society' when they reach the arbitrary age at which they are viewed as adults (Mitra & Gross, 2009, p. 526). This frustration is all too transparent in the case studies of the three Young Social Pioneers in Chapter 1. Its effects – young people's strong tendency to avoid or bypass the more formal or mainstream structures for civic and political participation – have already been described by Lucas Walsh and by James Arvanitakis and Eric Sidoti.

The mixed messages that surround young people extend and have their impact well beyond the schooling context, as other sections of this book explain, but they are particularly evident within it. Given the centrality of schools both in young people's lives and in the policy landscape in relation to young people, this is hardly an acceptable situation. Freire laid down the template for the educational endeavour when he wrote that 'one of the tasks of the progressive educator ... is to unveil opportunities for hope, no matter what the obstacles may be' (1994, p. 9). The obstacles to young people's participation are more than evident: it remains to be seen what opportunities for hope exist in our schools and for our young people.

References

Anderton, A., & Abbott, R. (2009). *Youth engagement – Deliberative research.* London: Youth Citizenship Commission.

Angus, L. (2006). 'Educational leadership and the imperative of including student voices, student interests, and students' lives in the mainstream'. *International Journal of Leadership in Education, 9*(4), 369–379.

Apple, M. W. (2002). Pedagogy, patriotism, and democracy: On the educational meanings of 11 September 2001. *Discourse: Studies in the Cultural Politics of Education, 23*(3), 299–308.

Apple, M. W. (2004). Schooling, markets, and an audit culture. *Educational Policy, 18*(4), 614–621.

Bennett, W. L., Wells, C., & Rank, A. (2008). *Young citizens and civic learning: Two paradigms of citizenship in the digital age. A report from the Civic Learning Online Project.* Seattle: Centre for Communication & Civic Engagement.

Bentley, T. (2002). *Learning beyond the classroom.* Seminar Series Paper 118, October 2002. Melbourne: Centre for Strategic Education.

Benton, T., Cleaver, E., Featherstone, G., Kerr, D., Lopes, J., & Whitby, K. (2008). *Young people's civic participation in and beyond school: Attitudes, intentions and influences. Citizenship Education Longitudinal Study (CELS): Sixth Annual Report.* Nottingham: National Foundation for Educational Research.

Bessant, J. (2004). Mixed messages: Youth participation and democratic practice. *Australian Journal of Political Science, 39*(2), 387–404.

Biesta, G. J. J. (2010). *Good education in an age of measurement: Ethics, politics, democracy.* Boulder: Paradigm Publishers.

Black, R. (2007). *Crossing the bridge: Overcoming entrenched disadvantage through student-centred learning.* Melbourne: Education Foundation Australia.

Black, R. (2008a). *Beyond the classroom: Building new school networks.* Melbourne: ACER Press.

Black, R. (2008b). *New school ties: Networks for success.* Office for Policy, Research and Innovation Paper No. 15, October 2008. Melbourne: Department of Education and Early Childhood Development.

Black, R. (2009). *Boardroom to classroom: The role of the corporate and philanthropic sectors in school education.* Office for Policy, Research and Innovation Paper No. 17, May 2009. Melbourne: Department of Education and Early Childhood Development.

Black, R., Stokes, H., Turnbull, M., & Levy, J. (2009). 'Civic participation through the curriculum'. *Youth Studies Australia, 28*(3), pp. 13–20

Black, R., & Walsh, L. (2009). *Corporate Australia and schools: Forming business class alliances and networks.* Seminar Series Paper 182, February 2009. Melbourne: Centre for Strategic Education.

Bragg, S. (2001). Taking a joke: Learning from the voices we don't want to hear. *Forum, 43*(2), 70–73.

Bragg, S. (2007). 'But I listen to children anyway!'—Teacher perspectives on pupil voice. *Educational Action Research, 15*(4), 505–518.

Brown, K., Lipsig-Mumme, C., & Zajdow, G. (2003). *Active citizenship and the secondary school experience: Community participation rates of Australian youth.* Melbourne: Australian Council for Educational Research.

Cairns, L. (2001). Investing in children: Learning how to promote the rights of all children. *Children and Society, 15*(5), 347–360.

Civics Expert Group (CEG). (1994). *Whereas the people ... Civics and citizenship education.* Report of the Civics Expert Group. Canberra: Australian Government Publishing Service.

Cleaver, E., Ireland, E., Kerr, D., & Lopes, J. (2005). *Citizenship education longitudinal study: Second cross-sectional survey 2004. Listening to young people: Citizenship education in England.* (DfES Research Report 626). London: Department for Education and Skills.

Collin, P. (2008). *Young people imagining a new democracy: Literature review.* Sydney: Whitlam Institute.

Cook-Sather, A. (2006). Sound, presence, and power: 'Student voice' in educational research and reform. *Curriculum Inquiry, 36*(4), 359–390.

Corbett, D., & Wilson, B. (1995). Make a difference with, not for, students: A plea to researchers and reformers. *Educational Researcher, 24*(5), 12–17.

Curriculum Corporation. (2006). *Statements of learning for civics and citizenship.* Melbourne: Curriculum Corporation.

Danby, S., & Farrell, A. (2004). Accounting for young children's competence in educational research: New perspectives on research ethics. *The Australian Educational Researcher, 31*(3), 35–49.

Davies, I., Flanagan, B., Hogarth, S., Mountford, P., & Philpott, J. (2009). Asking questions about participation. *Education, Citizenship and Social Justice, 4*(1), 25–39.

Davies, L. (2009). Educating against extremism: Towards a critical politicisation of young people. *International Review of Education, 55,* 183–203.

Department of Education, Science and Training. (2005). *National framework for values education in Australian schools.* Canberra: Commonwealth of Australia.

Department of Immigration and Citizenship. (2009). *I am Australian: Exploring Australian citizenship.* Canberra: Commonwealth of Australia.

Fielding, M. (2001). Students as radical agents of change. *Journal of Educational Change, 2*(3), 123–141.

Freire, P. (1994). *Pedagogy of hope: Reliving pedagogy of the oppressed.* New York: Continuum.

Giroux, H. A. (1990). Critical theory and the politics of culture and voice: Rethinking the discourse of educational research. In R. R. Sherman & R. B. Webb (Eds.), *Qualitative research in education: Focus and methods.* London: The Falmer Press.

Gunter, H., & Thomson, P. (2007). Learning about student voice. *Support for Learning, 22*(4), 181–188.

Hadfield, M., & Haw, K. (2001). 'Voice', young people and action research. *Educational Action Research, 9*(3), 485–502.

Harris, A., Wyn, J., & Younes, S. (2008). *Rethinking youth citizenship: Identity and connection*. Melbourne: Australian Youth Research Centre.

Holdsworth, R. (2000). Schools that create real roles of value for young people. *Prospects, XXX*(3), 349–362.

Johnson, K. (2004). *Children's voices: Pupil leadership in primary schools*. Nottingham: National College for School Leadership.

Kahne, J. E., & Middaugh, E. (2008). *Democracy for some: The civic opportunity gap in high school*. Maryland: The Center for Information and Research on Civic Learning and Engagement.

Keating, J. (2009). *A new federalism in Australian education: A proposal for a national reform agenda*. Melbourne: The Foundation for Young Australians.

Keating, J. (2010). *Resourcing schools in Australia: A proposal for the restructure of public funding*. Melbourne: The Foundation for Young Australians.

Kimberley, M. (Ed.). (2010). *Inclusive approaches with young people. What Works Australia* series. Melbourne: The Foundation for Young Australians and Australian Youth Research Centre.

Lerner, R. M., Alberts, A. E., & Bobek, D. L. (2007). *Thriving youth, flourishing civil society: A report for the Carl Bertelsmann-Prize 2007*. Bertelsmann Stiftung.

Levin, B. (2000). Putting students at the centre in education reform. *Journal of Educational Change, 1*(2), 155–172.

Mellor, S., & Kennedy, K. J. (2003). Australian students' democratic values and attitudes towards participation: Indicators from the IEA civic education study. *International Journal of Educational Research, 39*(6), 525–537.

Mellor, S., Kennedy, K. J., & Greenwood, L. (2001). *Citizenship and democracy: Australian students' knowledge and beliefs. The IEA civic education study of fourteen year olds*. Canberra: Commonwealth of Australia

Ministerial Council on Education, Employment, Training and Youth Affairs (MCEETYA). (2008). *Melbourne Declaration on Educational Goals for Young Australians*. Retrieved March 2011 from: http://www.mceecdya.edu.au/mceecdya/melbourne_declaration,25979.html

Ministerial Council on Education, Employment, Training and Youth Affairs. (MCEETYA) (2009). *National Assessment Program – Civics and Citizenship Years 6 and 10 Report 2007*. Carlton South: Ministerial Council on Education, Employment, Training and Youth Affairs.

Mitra, D. L. (2006). Increasing student voice and moving toward youth leadership. *The Prevention Researcher, 13*(1), 7–10.

Mitra, D. L., & Gross, S. J. (2009). Increasing student voice in high school reform: Building partnerships, improving outcomes. *Educational Management Administration & Leadership, 37*(4), 522–543.

Muir, K., Mullan, K., Powell, A., Flaxman, S., Thompson, D., & Griffiths, M. (2009). *State of Australia's young people: A report on the social, economic, health and family lives of young people.* Canberra: Australian Government.

Nudzor, H. P. (2009). Re-conceptualising the paradox in policy implementation: A post-modernist conceptual approach. *Discourse: Studies in the Cultural Politics of Education, 30*(4), 501–513.

Perry, L. B. (2009). Conceptualizing education policy in democratic societies. *Educational Policy, 23*(3), 423–450.

Print, M. (2007). Citizenship education and youth participation in democracy. *British Journal of Educational Studies, 55*(3), 325–345.

Raby, R. (2008). Frustrated, resigned, outspoken: Students' engagement with school rules and some implications for participatory citizenship. *International Journal of Children's Rights, 16,* 77–98.

Rasmussen, M. L., & Harwood, V. (2009). Young people, education and unlawful non-citizenship: Spectral sovereignty and governmentality in Australia. *Globalisation, Societies and Education, 7*(1), 5–22.

Reid, A., Cranston, N., Keating, J., & Mulford, B. (2010). Exploring the public purposes of education in Australian primary schools, Draft report of an ARC Linkage Project.

Rudduck, J., & Demetriou, H. (2003). Student perspectives and teacher practices: The transformative potential. *McGill Journal of Education, 38*(2), 274–288.

Smyth, J. (2006). Schools and communities put at a disadvantage: Relational power, resistance, boundary work and capacity building in educational identity formation. *Learning Communities: International Journal of Learning in Social Contexts, 3,* 7–49.

Spring, K., Dietz, N., & Grimm, R. (2007). *Youth helping America. Leveling the path to participation: Volunteering and civic engagement among youth from disadvantaged circumstances.* Washington: Corporation for National and Community Service.

Taylor, C., & Robinson, C. (2009). Student voice: Theorising power and participation. *Pedagogy, Culture & Society, 17*(2), 161–175.

Taylor, F. (Ed.). (2010a). *Partnerships in the youth sector. What Works Australia* series. Melbourne: The Foundation for Young Australians and Australian Youth Research Centre.

Taylor, F. (Ed.). (2010b). *Young people active in communities. What Works Australia* series. Melbourne: The Foundation for Young Australians and Australian Youth Research Centre.

Taylor, N., Smith, A. B., & Gollop, M. (2008). New Zealand children and young people's perspectives on citizenship. *International Journal of Children's Rights, 16*, 195–210.

Thomson, P. (2002). *Schooling the rustbelt kids: Making the difference in changing times.* Sydney: Allen & Unwin.

Thomson, P., & Holdsworth, R. (2003). Theorizing change in the educational 'field': Re-readings of 'student participation' projects. *International Journal of Leadership in Education, 6*(4), 371–391.

Thornberg, R. (2009). Rules in everyday school life: Teacher strategies undermine pupil participation. *International Journal of Children's Rights, 17*, 393–413.

Torney-Purta, J., Lehmann, R., Oswald, H., & Schulz, W. (2001). *Citizenship and education in twenty-eight countries: Knowledge and engagement at age fourteen.* Amsterdam: International Association for the Evaluation of Educational Achievement.

Walsh, L., & Black, R. (2009). *Students in the lead: Increasing participation by young people in a distributed leadership framework.* Seminar Series Paper 188, September 2009. Melbourne: Centre for Strategic Education.

Walsh, L., & Salvaris, M. (1998). What qualities of citizenship should Australian schools emphasise? In J. Smyth, R. Hattam & M. Lawson (Eds.), *Schooling for a fair go* (pp. 27–48). Sydney: The Federation Press.

Watts, R. J., & Flanagan, C. A. (2007). Pushing the envelope on youth civic engagement: A developmental and liberation psychology perspective. *Journal of Community Psychology, 35*(6), 779–792.

Westheimer, J., & Kahne, J. E. (2003). Reconnecting education to democracy: Democratic dialogues. *Phi Delta Kappan, 85(*1), 9–14.

Whitty, G., & Wisby, E. (2007). Whose voice? An exploration of the current policy interest in pupil involvement in school decision-making. *International Studies in Sociology of Education, 17*(3), 303–319.

Wierenga, A. (2003). *Sharing a new story: Young people in decision-making.* Melbourne: The Foundation for Young Australians and Australian Youth Research Centre.

Wilson, S. (2000). Schooling for democracy. *Youth Studies Australia, 19*(2), 25–31.

Wyn, J. (2009). Touching the future: Building skills for life and work. *Australian Education Review, 55*. Melbourne: Australian Council for Educational Research.

Wyn, J., & Woodman, D. (2006). Generation, youth and social change in Australia. *Journal of Youth Studies, 9*(5), 495–514.

New steps
to change

CHAPTER   3

Viewpoint 3:

Steps towards change

Thom Woodroofe

These days there are more opportunities than ever before for young Australians to be involved in their communities and most people would probably think they have been given an effective voice.

We are blessed to live in a democracy where young people can discuss and challenge government policy, start their own organisations and ultimately follow their passions whatever they may be.

But despite this, Australia still has a long way to go in supporting young people to be involved in their communities and in truly allowing their voices to be heard.

A desire to see Australia as a country that seeks and embraces the ideas of young people has formed the basis of my journey over the last few years. This is a journey I share collectively with young people across the country who are becoming involved in civic society and are out to make a difference – stretching from Cape York to Hobart; from Perth to Sydney; from the most remote communities to the inner suburbs of the cities.

But for me the concept of being involved in my community has changed dramatically throughout my life. It has grown from localised sporting activities to establishing a national organisation dedicated to harnessing and promoting the voices of young people. The journey has been an important one, showing me the breadth of passionate young people out there, eager to have their voices heard if given the right opportunity.

A journey starts with a step

As a young boy growing up in the country, becoming involved meant signing up with the local football team during winter and the local cricket team during summer. I would brave wintry weekend mornings to kick the football around a muddy oval and then brave blistering summer heat to stand on the field for hours waiting for the ball to be hit toward me. Like most kids, my sense of being involved was very much about getting to know and having fun with those in my local town.

As the seasons dragged on, though, my thoughts shifted from being purely about the game and having fun, to thinking about how the club could be changed or how the training sessions could be overhauled. On one level this was just the process of becoming older and the maturity of the thought process, which may or may not have been underscored by my distinct lack of goals or runs! But nevertheless I started to develop a 'voice' of ideas and concepts about my community, even if I lacked the outlet for them, much wider than simply trying to get the ball or score as many runs as possible.

As I got older, though, my sense of wanting to become involved grew to encompass much more than my local town, and my sense of community inevitably grew. When I turned 12 and started high school I joined the Australian Air Force Cadets, a national youth organisation that provides leadership training and development to teenagers. Admittedly, this was a strange progression for a rural farm boy, but one that provided me innumerable opportunities over the years that followed.

While many of my peers would spend their weekends studying, catching up with friends or partying, I spent a large portion of my teenagehood putting in the hard yards on the parade ground, in the bush and in the air. The environment, culture and character of the organisation infected me, and I felt a strong sense of both belonging and identity doing activities that most teenagers do not ordinarily get the opportunity to do.

It was an interesting experience for me. On one hand, it provided me with the opportunity to develop as an individual in so many facets of life, but on the other the regimented nature of the military culture stifled much of my own flair for opinion and a voice. The notion of community for me had certainly expanded beyond my local geography, but was still bounded by the activities and operations of an organisation and its inherent culture.

2007 was very much a turning point for me. That year, I was appointed as the senior Air Force Cadet for Australia, a position that brought with it a great deal of responsibility and commitment for a 17-year-old. I moved into a largely administrative role with two core functions: to canvass the opinions and ideas of the 6500 members across the country and secondly to represent those views to the upper echelons of the organisation.

It was a demanding role indeed. Almost every weekend I was away interstate and by the end of the year I had missed half of the school calendar (though I did very well, to the surprise of my teachers). But it was an incredibly inspiring and motivating year for many reasons.

That year I met thousands of teenagers across the country, from different backgrounds and walks of life. I experienced what is most beautiful about our country and also what is most confronting. There were young people on Thursday Island who were putting aside their isolation from the mainland and starting a local cadet unit, there were young people who were learning to fly before they could drive, and there were young people becoming trained peer counsellors after experiencing hardship themselves. In each and every way, these young people were active, engaged and incredibly motivated to be involved with their communities.

To them and me, however, community wasn't just people in their local unit: it was anyone who wore the uniform across the country. Each of these young people had their own story, something to say both through their actions and through their words when asked, and I was touched by how eager they were to express it if only given the chance.

Turning an idea into a reality

At the start of 2008, after moving to the city for university and leaving cadets, I felt like I drifted for several months without a sense of involvement. It was a difficult time for me and I dipped my feet in many of the organisations giving young people a voice, but couldn't find what I was looking for. I was eager to participate in so many ways.

It was then that I conceptualised what has ultimately become Left Right Think-Tank, Australia's first independent and non-partisan think-tank of young minds. In essence, I wanted to create a platform for young people aged 15 to 25 who were passionate about a particular topic but lacked the networks or resources to research and drive it further.

It was my experience that young people were sick of partisan politics and eager to focus on the substance of ideas. The constant mud-slinging and sound bite approach to topics was increasingly repugnant to a generation confronted by some of the greatest challenges to the environment, the economy and many other parts of the society in which their children would be born.

All of the research at the time suggested that young people were just as involved as they had ever been, but that the paradigm had shifted from university movements to more entrepreneurial forms of participation and greater reach across the community. In other words, young people weren't just limiting themselves to university clubs or movements fuelled by campus politics but were out there in the wider community following their passions and, in some instances, starting their own projects or organisations.

Alongside this, they were shifting in their political involvement, becoming more 'cause focused' on particular issues or passions. But there was a distinct lack of opportunity for young people to be able to contribute to these causes and issues, outside of what were regarded as 'youth issues'. These were issues that were seen as directly affecting young people and were typically, and often negatively, associated with their generation – binge drinking, loitering, skate park locations and so forth. What was missing was the outlet for young people's voices to be heard much more widely – for young people with great passions and a willingness to learn and engage to join the debates on the economy, the environment, foreign affairs, or even nanotechnology.

In my opinion, Left Right was an idea whose time had come, but that didn't make it an organic process. The year that followed was the toughest I have ever experienced. Despite our positive mission, we were amazed by the sheer number of hurdles that seemed to be constantly placed in our path.

There were those that doubted us and there were those that simply did not support us for whatever reason. It was a year of exhilarating highs and exasperating lows as our eyes opened to the culture that surrounded youth participation in this country.

But surmounting all this was the enormous groundswell of interest we experienced from young people echoing our values and eager to get involved. By mid-2009, just over a year later, as an organisation we had grown across four states – from Victoria, to New South Wales, up to Queensland and across to Western Australia. In these states we had rolled out highly successful programs on the ground like regular dialogue-based events, a comprehensive hard core policy development cycle, and a training program for high-school students about how policy is made in Australia.

The culture of youth participation

It is ironic, but many of the barriers we experienced in establishing Left Right were in fact driven by the proliferation of the term 'young people'. It is unfortunate, but these days 'young people' is a buzzword thrown around as much as 'disadvantaged' or 'marginalised' and not always for the right reasons.

It is my firm belief that the effectiveness of youth participation and engagement is not measured by the number of people involved, or even the level to which they are involved, but by the extent to which their involvement can drive and influence real change. While there are certainly more opportunities for young people to be engaged in their communities than ever before, meaningful opportunities are starving for air in an increasingly polluted environment of tokenism.

1985 was a turning point for the evolution of youth participation. This was four years before I was even born, but its importance to my work today and of so many others my age could not have been more central.

Against the backdrop of International Youth Year, the term 'young people' matured into a fully-fledged categorisation in political and social discourse. Almost overnight, young people went from being teenagers and adults participating in society to 'young people' with a category of their own until they reached 25. They suddenly became a band of society that needed special attention and programs that were seen to be delivering that attention. Initiatives specifically targeted at youth sprang up from government, business and the wider community. Suddenly, young people were no longer everyday citizens but a group that had to play in the corner in a special section.

In other words, while this categorisation as young people has led to more opportunities, it has also prevented participation at the 'big table' in many ways by creating a culture of 'waiting your turn at the little table'.

The reality is that young people should be valued as everyday citizens and given opportunities to participate in meaningful ways. And just as there is a burden of responsibility on us all to ensure the opportunities are meaningful, there is a similar burden on the young to show their involvement is worthwhile and actually producing dividends.

Too often the temptation is to agree to attractive titles that might disguise the tokenistic nature of the role, whether it is on a local youth council or an advisory board to a bank. The real question is: how many of these opportunities are actually about driving change? Too often this sort of involvement of young people results in no change whatsoever – unless it is driven by the young people themselves in a supportive environment.

Roger Hart (1992) proposed a ladder that symbolises young people's participation in society. Dare I say it in the post-Latham era, this is somewhat of a Ladder of Opportunity. The ladder analogy is also a good visual representation, highlighting the dominance of tokenistic youth participation in society and the scarcity of effective models of youth and adult collaboration.

Hart breaks down the roles young people can play in society into eight distinct groups, or rungs, on the ladder. It starts with the manipulation of young people's involvement before eventually reaching the dizzy heights of shared decision-making and the initiation of change.

The first three categories – manipulation, decoration and tokenism – reflect what has elsewhere been called 'adultism', which in broad terms refers to the discrimination against young people simply for not being adults. All three occur when adult causes are cast as youth programs, varying from those that are manipulated to seem as though they are actually driven by young people to those that involve young people but don't give them a voice in the process.

Above these are categories Hart describes as 'assigned but informed' and 'consulted and informed' participation. These are perhaps the middle ground most often seen in Australia, where young people are either assigned a specific task or asked for their opinion, such as on a community youth board, or asked to funnel their opinions and suggestions into an 'adult' forum rather than being directly involved with that adult forum, such as the relationship a youth council might have with the local council.

The top three rungs of Hart's ladder, beginning with adult-initiated shared decisions with young people, and culminating in youth-initiated, shared decisions with adults, are where Australia needs to climb. They exemplify young people's roles as citizens through either adult-initiated but youth-run projects, or the top rung of youth-led activism that is supported by adults through assistance and effective mentoring.

Australia already has some wonderful examples of this type of youth-led change. At the macro-level, organisations like the United Nations Youth Association of Australia, Oaktree Foundation, Australian Youth Climate Coalition, National Union of Students and Left Right Think-Tank are working every day to achieve outcomes they are as passionate about as young people themselves. There is a lot that can be learned from the way these organisations approach youth engagement and partnership-driven models with others in the community.

At the micro-level there are countless examples of young people being supported by adults to create change, through local recycling campaigns or in discouraging street violence. Sometimes young people are the best agency to address problems within their age group or to drive awareness on issues, often in the most creative of ways. An example is an emerging group called Step Back Think, founded by a close friendship group in the wake of the bashing of one of their friends to a vegetative state on the streets of Melbourne. This group of young people is simply trying to change attitudes to alcohol and violence among other young people, to stop them going through the pain and suffering they and their friend have experienced.

Towards a culture of citizenship

The culture of youth participation in Australia is all over the road and in dire need of a service. On one hand, there are meaningful opportunities that should be encouraged: young people running for councils, starting organisations and businesses, or even just running a local recycling campaign. Anything that will create positive social change! And on the other, there are those activities that are seen as encouraging young people but which are more about corporate self-interest and ticking a checkbox in a corporate social responsibility strategy, and which result in no change whatsoever through the involvement of young people.

In order for us to truly value the voices of young people, we need to move towards a culture that is defined by their citizenship, not by social categories. It is my hope that, as a country, we can move beyond blindly encouraging more young people to be involved in their communities or seeking their input whenever we feel we should. Instead, we need to focus on best supporting young people to discover their passions and, once they do, supporting them to create positive social change in whatever way possible – through money, mentoring, encouragement and networks.

Government has possibly the most important role to play in this progression. The way that government treats young people, either as a select social category or as a group that spans every demographic like other citizens but who are simply young in age, is critical. In that sense, young people should not just be included in one aspect of government, but across portfolios. Government should not view its role as a 'creator' but as a supporter of young people's participation. This would not only limit the burden of bureaucracy on government as it became involved with youth participation, but help support best practice already out there by embracing a social marketplace model of youth enterprise.

My journey so far has taught me one important lesson: when young people become involved, they are the most powerful catalyst for change in society, whether it is the way their football club runs or the direction their country is taking. By challenging negative stereotypes and linking their passion to areas of involvement, young people will become empowered by their own voices, and this cycle of empowerment and social change becomes self-perpetuating.

Ultimately, creating meaningful opportunities for young people to discover their passions and to drive change is the challenge for all of us, and something I hope to engage with on my journey ahead.

References

Hart, R. A. (1992). Children's participation: From tokenism to citizenship. *Innocenti Essays*, No. 4. UNICEF International Child Development Centre. Retrieved 2 March 2011 from: http://www.unicef-irc.org/publications/pdf/childrens_participation.pdf

Thom Woodroofe was the 2009 Young Victorian of the Year and founder of Left Right Think-Tank, Australia's first independent and non-partisan think-tank of young minds.

Case study 3:

SYN

The Student Youth Network Inc., better known as SYN, is a youth-run media organisation that provides training and broadcast opportunities for young Australians aged between 12 and 25 years, offering them the skills and platforms to be creators and not just consumers of media. According to Georgia Webster, General Manager, SYN's primary purpose as a social enterprise is to provide young people with the opportunity to be heard: 'we train young people to facilitate their stories, their ideas, their perspectives, their cultures'.

SYN was formed in 2000 as a merger between the Student Radio Association and 3TD AM, a youth radio station run by students from Thornbury-Darebin Secondary College. It was awarded a Melbourne-wide FM community radio broadcasting licence in 2001, in the face of strong competition from other broadcasters and before permanent broadcasting commenced in 2003. That same year, SYN TV was launched and simulcast on radio and the internet as the first television program to be hosted exclusively by young people under the age of 18. In 2010, the SYN website was revamped and re-launched to take full advantage of the vast array of social networking and media sharing tools available, helping it to reach a larger proportion of its target demographic.

Former SYNner and 'biographer' of SYN, Ellie Rennie has observed that 'for all the talk of a new communications paradigm there are very few stories of the people who are actually experiencing it' (2009, p. 4). The story of SYN is an exception, and the advantage of digital technology and information and communication technologies (ICTs) for this particular youth organisation is obvious. The broadcasting process itself calls for familiarity with technology, with young people chaperoned through a hands-on training process in which they learn to use a radio panel and a microphone, and to record an interview over the phone. Beyond these fundamental skills, a familiarity with online technology is imperative for participation at SYN. A solid web presence offers a cheap, appealing and effective way to connect with audiences in Australia and overseas.

The process of building this web presence has required some adjustment along the way. The former General Manager of SYN, Bryce Ives, focused on the potential of SYN's website from the beginning of his term and, mindful of the shift toward ICTs, made the difficult decision to axe SYN's only paper publication, *Pecado*. Under his supervision a web redevelopment project began in late 2006, with the aim of building social networking capacity into SYN's site, but technology shifted so dramatically in two years that the project lost its relevance. It was abandoned in favour of something 'simpler', says the current General Manager: 'a publication point for SYN volunteers, schools we work with and young people … we want a spot for them to put their media, and also a seamless interaction with other social networks that our communities of interest, potential audiences, might be existing in'.

Today, SYN radio and TV program hosts can use specially allocated pages for promotion and to post video and audio content. The site allows for the creation of interest groups to discuss particular subjects and is 'pretty nuanced in how you can search for stuff', according to Georgia. She explains: 'Some shows are using it for texts, writing blog posts … It also embeds across from YouTube and external video hosting sites. It can post pretty nice little links through to Facebook and that kind of thing'. Site designers used open-source technology, and the minimal cost of setting up the website has been more than compensated for by the scope of its impact. Google Analytics provides exact figures on who is using the site, when and where. Traffic to the new site increased by 50 per cent in its first three months of operation in 2010. With a goal of 800 to 1000 hits a day, the site is already receiving 500 and at the time of writing regularly reaches 1000 on Tuesday's very popular Asian Pop Night. Broadening the site and making it fully compatible with mobile devices Georgia considers will not be 'as big a hurdle as getting a radio licence and fundraising a million bucks for a transmitter … it's not about money, it's about time in this new ICT space'.

Where once the whole make-up of SYN may have been regarded as haphazard – the constant turnover of program hosts in keeping with the station's age restrictions, the dishevelled share house atmosphere of its studios, the lack of adherence to censorship guidelines, and the willingness to take on any young person with an idea regardless of experience – it now looks positively progressive. Rennie notes that '"squatting and claiming" has gone from something marginal and derisible to a legitimate force that must now be taken seriously' (2009, p. 13) Albeit with a recent facelift, this has been SYN's modus operandi since it first began. Rennie remembers:

During my time there, social networking became the most popular use of the internet and traditional media institutions were forced to acknowledge the rise of amateur content. SYN rethought its approach to the online environment. They killed their print publication, dealt with the introduction of digital broadcasting and taught school teachers about a new kind of literacy. In just two years, dozens of careers were launched. The SYN radio audience doubled. And they got told off for swearing.

(2009, p. 4)

Jane Ryan has hosted SYN radio's current affairs program *Panorama* as well as *Get Cereal TV*, and is newsreader for Channel 31's motorsports program, *In Pit Lane*. Elaborating on the benefits of ICTs for program presenters she claims that 'a lot of the interaction you get between listeners and presenters is via chat rooms or via a live chat website facilitated by the SYN website, and then also of course by phone, text message, all that sort of stuff'. She concedes that the internet as a communication tool is 'really important because everything is orchestrated … via social networking sites'. In addition, the SYN site includes a password-protected billboard where producers, hosts and crew members can offer tips to one another 'on how to operate within the technical spectrum better … people can post ideas, comment on previous shows, approach each other in areas where certain people have strengths and others don't'.

With the advent of digital broadcasting, Georgia claims that SYN will be providing a corresponding online stream 'to offset that question of "who's going to listen [when] the radios cost $300?" We're really focused on having that online to ensure that it's readily available'. In theory, digital broadcasting has the potential to make SYN's programs more accessible by packaging them into sound bites and podcasts, not only useful for its young listeners but for public commentators and politicians wanting to tap into the 'youth voice'. Just how much attention policy-makers are paying to the SYNners, however, is up for debate. The station is supported by funding from both state and federal governments – such as the Department of Education, Employment and Workplace Relations' Youth Development and Support Program – and is represented on the Australian Youth Forum steering committee, but the impact of its programs in the broader political landscape is difficult to measure. Jane sees SYN's role 'primarily as an educator and not as a medium for young people to have their voices heard in the political arena':

I'd go further than that and I'd say that I think that youth affairs seems to have come to a bit of a standstill in terms of having a great student body that is articulating youth issues because, more and more, the harder it is to get into a role in the media or in public life, the earlier people have to start trying. So people approach these arenas with very certain objectives and agendas. You might have a student union president at a university whose real agenda is not necessarily to represent their demographic with passion, but to promote their own career as a politician or in the public eye. Similarly, I think that quite often the target audience for the people who are using SYN is … future employers … and I think that's good as well. It's really amazing to have that opportunity.

After several years observing operations at SYN, Rennie too began to question the position of SYN as a 'platform for young people – a means for an excluded group to have a voice' but concluded that this did not necessarily matter: 'When I first encountered SYN I assumed it was designed for that purpose. But the fact is that the SYNners have not experienced exclusion from the public sphere in the same way as my generation (X, that is)'. She notes that 'an alternative has always been there for the Y kids. And exclusion doesn't mean much when there are other, more exciting places to be'.

Despite this, Jane is adamant that 'a really important role that SYN plays in the community for young people is that it gives them confidence, and it gives them the feeling that they are being heard – even if they're not':

I think that children and young people who feel listened to are more likely to behave in a way that will bring about change, and that it's the disenfranchisement and disillusion of young people who don't feel like anyone [cares] that can't effect change in a positive way for their community. They feel defeated, whereas these kids really feel like there's an opportunity for them to make a difference, even if it's on a very small level. I think that has significant impact on their mentality.

For her part, Georgia acknowledges that 'policy impact is [n]ever going to be a primary goal of SYN, but I like to think that the space it has created can lead to more understanding of those nuances and youth perspectives and that will hopefully have a positive impact'. In her view the role of community media as a training ground for mainstream media is 'pretty overplayed'.

Doubtless the opinion around or hope for SYN's impact shifts depending on the program in question. Some hosts aim simply to entertain, or give airtime and credibility to an obscure type of music. In their own way, Georgia observes, 'some of those cultural things have the potential to change a whole range of ideas'. For young political commentators like Jane, the station may operate less as a mouthpiece for Australian youth and more as a translation service with presenters as the 'conduit … the link between the older demographic of media and the powers that be, and the youth':

> Rather than finding information that's been filtered through websites designed for youth, it's quite often people who have chosen to take on the role of presenter or producer or commentator that have to trawl through the information presented to the adult community and then translate it for the young people who are listening. So for me, I would do a spot on the SYN program Get Cereal TV, I'd go on for seven minutes once a week and I would do a breakdown of one issue in politics for that week. And I wasn't taking my information from a government education website or a wiki pool or a youth forum. It was because I had done a lot of research into, say, double dissolution elections, and then I would go on and turn it into something fun and cute and sexy and great that people want to listen to and people can actually compute.

As for the school kids who get the chance to take up a little airtime with something less well-prepared, 'I think that they're shaking their tail feather, you know. They're really streets ahead of any other kids their age who have never even imagined doing something like that'.

Georgia agrees that 'having someone hear their voice and what they've got to say for 10 minutes is something that's never happened to them before. They've never had that sense that there's a few thousand people out there listening to them'. Jane remembers:

> I used to listen to Triple J as a teenager, I used to just think that they were completely untouchable. They were just so far removed and they were so impossibly cool and I was just awestruck with the prospect of ever being on the radio. I guess crossing that barrier for me, because I did it when I was older and I'd had life experience that led to me understanding how not rock star-esque that whole arena is, it was a little bit less shiny for me. But I think definitely for kids that

age who can tell their friends to tune in on Tuesday afternoon and hear them do a comedy sketch – it's just a total knockout.

References

Rennie, E. (2009). *Life of SYN: A Story of the Digital Generation.* Melbourne: unpublished manuscript. Cited with permission of the author.

Interview with Georgia Webster (Barbara Lemon), 14 April 2010.

Interview with Jane Ryan (Barbara Lemon), 14 April 2010.

Commentary 3:

Emergent forms and tools of change-making

Lucas Walsh

Introduction

Previously, in Chapter 1, I explored the challenges and possibilities for inclusion, engagement and participation within and via conventional channels and institutions, such as schools, through voting and other civic activities. New forms and methods of change-making are emerging that are both youth-led and which seek to benefit young people. This commentary provides an introductory overview of two of these: social enterprises and the use of information and communication technologies (ICTs). It explores new ways that young people are connecting with each other and seeking to make change in a shifting landscape.

I start by outlining the nature of social enterprises, which have emerged with a particular emphasis on young people and as a dynamic and influential means for making change. Drawing from the case study of one social enterprise, SYN FM, this commentary explores the ways in which young people and organisations seeking to benefit youth are using ICTs to connect with each other both across and in between conventional spaces of engagement, communication and participation. To set the context for this, a brief overview is provided of the technological shift in attitude and tools from the initial development of the web to what is often referred to as Web 2.0. This shift is characterised by a move from the one-way 'push' delivery of information, services and content from relatively selective providers, to the user-driven and highly dispersed environments of social networking that emerged as a result of Web 2.0 tools and thinking.

I then critically interrogate the degree to which ICTs are enabling genuine participation and change-making. In addition, persistent challenges in access and literacy continue to present barriers to the use of ICTs.

Understanding the emergence of social enterprises and the use of ICTs for communication, engagement and participation provides insight into a shifting environment in which young people can make change.

Young people and the emergence of social enterprises

During the last decade, a complex reconfiguration of the relationship of government, private corporations and civil society has begun that has enabled new opportunities and spaces for young people to engage in change-making on matters of importance to them. In this changing environment, young change-makers pick and sample from corporate, government and third-sector resources and approaches to create more agile organisational vehicles for making social impact. In the Foreword to this book, Cheryl Kernot highlights the emergence of social entrepreneurs who reject the assumption that governments and corporations can best determine the most effective allocation of resources. Their vehicles for change-making – social enterprises – typically seek to work in between the spaces typically occupied by government, philanthropy or corporate social responsibility. In 2010, it was estimated that there were about 20 000 Australian social enterprises with the most frequently targeted beneficiary being young people (Australian Centre for Philanthropy and Nonprofit Studies [ACPNS] & Social Traders, 2010, p. 24).

Crudely defined as a viable business with a social agenda, a social enterprise seeks to bring about positive social change. Social enterprises have been characterised as 'profit with purpose', 'social capital over hard assets', 'living better with less' and 'entrepreneurship as disruption'. Rather than replacing traditional charities or government, social enterprises tend to target unmet areas of need or gaps in service delivery, as the case study of OUTthere illustrates. Social enterprises seek to deliver social outcomes but are typically organised more like businesses. As Cheryl notes, they use traditional business tools to generate dividends that are reinvested in the core social purpose of the enterprise. Social enterprises may be profit-seeking, but they are never profit-maximising. Unlike businesses, delivering social outcomes is their primary reason for being (Saunders, 2010). In social enterprise, social impact takes priority over profit. While many draw on business and industry networks, they tend not to measure their bottom line in the same way that businesses do. They reinvest the majority of their profit or surplus back into the fulfilment of their mission (ACPNS & Social

Traders, 2010). So to businesses they look like charities, while to charities they look like businesses (Saunders, 2010).

The case studies of Young Social Pioneers in Chapter 1 illustrated the frustration of many young change-makers in the slowness of government process and hesitance with their processes and capacity to make timely, grassroots change. Social enterprises have grown as a result of a need for change-making to take place in more dynamic, responsive and efficient ways.

Young people, such as GetUp!'s national director, Simon Sheikh, are leading many of these social enterprises to make change. Organisations like GetUp! are exploiting the benefits of recent developments in ICTs. Using platforms and tools such as social networking and viral marketing, these technologies are being harnessed to make change and to communicate with online communities in ways that are difficult for many older people to fathom.

Innovation in technology, interaction and attitude

Before illustrating some of the ways that youth-oriented social enterprises are using ICTs, it is useful to understand the context of profound technological development during the last two decades. Great tides of technological innovation such as wikis, blogs, semantic web, relational databases, short message services (SMS), social networking, mobile phone applications and other networks have provided the tools and environments for varieties of human interaction and sharing of information. The internet and mobile telephony in particular have become truly ubiquitous.

The tools and environments that ICTs offer young people to participate and make change can be understood by examining two stages of web development, and the ways that this development has impacted on user engagement and interaction.

During its first stage of development, the web functioned primarily for the interchange of documents (W3C, 2007). The first stage of web development favoured a top-down approach to the delivery of information and services. Information was typically 'pushed' from an organisation to its audience. The Malian Foundation, for example, uses the web to provide products, services and support for charitable causes worldwide. Established in 2004 by 19-year-old Simon Malian, the organisation caters to charitable organisations with limited cash flow by supplying free management consulting services and software. The Foundation's site (www.malianfoundation.org) primarily uses

ICTs to disseminate information and tools. Oaktree Foundation, an aid and development organisation run by volunteers under 26 years old, uses its site to profile current events, promote international projects and invite donations and volunteers (www.theoaktree.org). The Enterprise Network for Young Australians (www.enya.org.au) similarly provides information about business practice without explicitly pushing a particular agenda for social change.

During the last decade, more applications and communication tools have became publicly available to extend the scope for online collaboration, social networking and sharing among users (Halavais, 2006, p. 1217). A shift has occurred away from the centralised provision of content, towards applications and services enabling users to take more control over how they create, access and share information. The growth of user-generated applications, tools and environments, such as wikis and blogs, reflects a longer-term trend in ICT use towards user-driven and diffuse online environments. Referred to as 'Web 2.0' (O'Reilly, 2005), this term is more of an 'attitude' than a technology (Davis, 2005). Coined in 2004 by Tim O'Reilly, the idea of Web 2.0 took shape following the end of the dot-com boom (Shannon, 2006). Underpinning the Web 2.0 attitude is a view of users as active and expressive beings. Young people in particular reflect this attitude by being less 'passive recipients of mass consumer culture', and more active users 'searching, reading, scrutinising, authenticating, collaborating, and organising' (Tapscott & Williams, 2006, p. 47). It emerged with the development of more open-ended, dynamic and user-friendly platforms and applications enabling easier sharing, organising and repurposing of different kinds of content.

Blog posts, for example, can be published, linked and subscribed to across a network (Spivack, 2003). Wiki tools enable relatively inexperienced users to quickly and easily publish to the web. (The word 'wiki' is taken from a Hawaiian word for 'fast'.) Online and mobile networking provides 'a fast and efficient method of changing public opinion through their ability to mobilise email and petition campaigns and raise funds for advertising campaigns for or against particular issues' (Murphy, 2008). Tweeting is a currently fashionable means of micro-blogging. Importantly, these tools enable content to be created collaboratively and shared. By enabling users to become creators of content, they continue to be very effective in facilitating greater individual and collective expression (Augar, Raitman & Zhou, 2006). Web 2.0 tools enable easier and greater interaction between organisations, content creators and users through consultations, petitions and collaborative platforms such as wikis and discussion forums.

Web 2.0 technologies provide opportunities for further engagement in social and political life. Perez (2008) provides some suggestions and examples of social media. Blogs, for example, are used to encourage people to donate to the Red Cross in support of earthquake victims. Short messaging via Twitter has enabled rapid fundraising for similar ends across vast social networks. Facebook is used to galvanise support for social causes. Social media can be used to connect families, enable emergency relief during disasters, and provide on-the-ground perspectives through citizen journalism and mobile activism. Sites such as MobileActive.org provide a community of volunteers and organisations to bring about social impact using mobile phones (Perez, 2008).

Young social entrepreneurs and ICTs

This technological shift offers particular benefits to social enterprise. It is important to remember that ICTs are not the drivers of social change: people are. The capacity of ICTs to be used for social change depends upon 'individual inventiveness and entrepreneurialism' (Castells, 2000, p. 5). Organisations have access to a growing number of ready-made tools and applications from which they can add value to their stakeholder engagement and increase their impact. ICTs appeal to social change organisations with limited communications budgets. As Schuler suggests, 'for the first time in human history, the possibility exists to establish a communication network that spans the globe, is affordable, and is open to all comers and points of view' (Schuler, 2003, p. 69). Many young change-makers use digital technologies as a fast and cost-effective way to assist in the administration of their organisations and build relationships with end-users, stakeholders and wider audiences. The plethora of free web-based tools and applications described above provide opportunities for organisations to add value in low-cost and inventive ways. For example, Project Australia's website offers resources and discussion forums for young social entrepreneurs. Launched in 2006, this not-for-profit social enterprise run by young Australians is seeking to use the web to provide access to mentors, case studies, templates, event listings and financial advice (www.projectaustralia.org.au).

For some social enterprises, digital media provide the primary tools and channels for social change. Make Believe (www.makebelieve.me) is a youth-run organisation that works predominantly online. Make Believe conducts online publicity campaigns, ranging from rallying support for Burma's pro-democracy leader Aung San Suu Kyi, to promoting the closure of the Guantanamo detention facility, to 'Go Home On Time Day', which seeks to raise awareness of unpaid overtime work. Make Believe uses viral marketing and tools such as online surveys, YouTube, and the strategic placement of banner advertising to communicate its messages.

The Australian Youth Climate Coalition (AYCC) is an example of a youth-led, youth-oriented enterprise that uses ICTs to enable human and resource mobilisation to engage young people in learning about and taking action in response to climate change. The AYCC uses its site (www.youthclimatecoalition.org) as a platform to: provide information about particular policy agendas, projects and campaigns, such as the development of a Green curriculum to educate young Australians about environmental sustainability; raise money for specific projects, such as sending Pacific Islander and Indigenous youth representatives to the United Nations; and to convene large groups of people to take action 'face-to-face'. The AYCC uses blogging, links to Facebook, Twitter applications and email alerts as a means to recruit volunteers and donate to the organisation.

While most social enterprises provide a point of contact on the web, increasing numbers of social enterprises like the AYCC tap into the vast networks enabled by social media. It is in the spirit of this second kind of interaction that websites are used as a means to foster active dialogue and engagement. The online strategies used by Vibewire Youth Inc. and ActNow are good examples of this. Vibewire Youth Inc. provides a range of forums for young artists, creative writers and journalists to share their work (http://vibewire.org/). An enterprise hub is available for aspiring young creative and social entrepreneurs. Another part of the site allows users to comment on news and events and share ideas. Aside from disseminating information and providing support for young people seeking to understand mental health issues, ActNow (www.actnow.com.au) provides young people with resources and tools to help them take action on issues of concern to them. Online forums, digital stories, podcasts and SMS campaigns are used to facilitate participation, dialogue and interaction with young people (Collin, 2008).

GetUp! (www.getup.org.au) has been particularly successful at conducting campaigns across different platforms, both online and off. GetUp! describes itself as an 'independent, grass-roots, community advocacy organisation'. Established in 2005, it attracted over 380 000 members by 2010. As Kathy Marks points out, this is a greater membership base than all three major political parties combined. Nearly one in 35 voters is a member of GetUp! (Marks, 2010, pp. 28–31). It claims to have had 'unprecedented success in campaigning outside the political and social institutions and uncovered a new constituency that has previously been kept out of or ignored by institution-developed processes' (Murphy, 2008). It sees itself as having played an important role in weakening some of the Howard government's hardline approaches to matters such as the abortion drug RU486 and the treatment of David Hicks. Known also for conducting multimedia campaigns targeting issues such as climate change, electoral reform, industrial relations, Indigenous affairs, same sex equality and voter enrolment, GetUp!'s public profile was especially high during the lead-up to the 2007 and 2010 federal elections; the latter of which they ran a targeted and successful campaign to reverse the Howard government's action in 2006 to close enrolments for new voters at 8pm on the day the election was officially announced.

ICTs are also used for subversive and disruptive activities such as hacking or flash mobbing, which seek to bring about change outside conventional, formal channels of engagement and decision-making. For example, political engagement through 'flash mobs' uses communications technology such as email or SMS via mobile phones to quickly mobilise a group of people to a particular place or collective action, such as a protest. Sometimes, mobs seek to do no more than protest through the satire of spontaneous performance.

The subversive, disruptive and often criminal activities of hackers and hacktivists are another, darker side of ICT use. Some of the world's first high-profile hackers were allegedly young Australians. During the 1980s and 1990s, a loosely formed group of hackers known as 'The Realm' were responsible for invading high-profile computer systems in Australia and the US, including the US Naval Research Laboratory. Their attacks played a central role in the creation of Australia's first federal cyber-crime legislation, created under pressure from the US government (Anderson, 2003; Dreyfus, 1997). It is believed that the notorious WANK worm (Worms Against Nuclear Killers) protest which caused mayhem for NASA scientists in 1989 may also have originated in Australia (*The New York Times*, 1999; Denning, 2004). The use of hacking for political ends is loosely referred to as Hacktivism, which uses digital tools and technical proficiency to exert political influence in legally ambiguous and illegal ways (*Wikipedia*, 2010; Samuel, 2004).

Web 2.0 technologies are appealing to young people seeking new, unregulated avenues of political influence and change-making. A major motivation for many young people to participate outside conventional political channels is summed up by Thao Nguyen, a Youth Representative for Australia speaking at the UN General Assembly in 2008:

Anything the government does to give young people a voice is all a token gesture, because they believe that youth don't have the capacity to make meaningful changes. So you either don't do anything, and just concentrate on interest rates, or you just bypass it and get involved in global organisations or networks where you actually feel you are making a difference.

(Stokes, Pitty & Smith, 2008, p. 190)

When successful, these technologies have been used to shift loci of power away from conventional channels and institutions of control, such as government or big business. By enabling a decentralised approach to communication, interaction, participation and content creation, the use of ICTs is attractive to social movements oriented towards 'diversity, decentralisation, informality and grassroots democracy' (van de Donk et al., 2004, p. 4).

ICTs and authentic participation

Web 2.0 technologies allow greater interactivity, networking and platforms. It is important to note, however, that greater interactivity and collective engagement does not necessarily translate to sustained social and political impact. Despite the hyperbole and hysteria, there is surprisingly little solid evidence that ICTs play a major role in producing agentic, deliberate change in a sustained way. The question of whether the kinds of participation outlined above are 'real' or 'fake' is a contemporary manifestation of an older, fundamental question as to what constitutes 'authentic' participation. Widespread use of the term 'participation', observed Pateman (1972, p. 1), 'has tended to mean that any precise, meaningful content has almost disappeared; "participation" is used to refer to a wide variety of different situations by different people'.

In digital environments, interactivity is sometimes confused with participation. Communications scholars in the area of technology and political engagement are therefore careful to differentiate access and interaction from participation, as these first two elements of political engagement do not in themselves constitute authentic participation (Cammaerts & Carpentier, 2005). When thinking about the use of something like Facebook in a campaign to raise awareness about a given issue, it is important to remember that Facebook enables interaction between campaigners and social networks to encourage people to consider and, if necessary, act on the issue. As such, becoming a Facebook friend of a given issue is part of an interaction rather than participation. The kinds of point-click activism by those who show support for a social cause by doing nothing other than updating their Facebook status or joining an online group is regarded as pseudo-participation, sometimes colloquially labelled as 'slacktivism' (Ma, 2009).

For Servaes (1999, p. 198), authentic participation 'directly addresses power and its distribution in society. It touches the very core of power relationships'. Pateman differentiates full participation from a process of partial participation, 'in which two or more parties influence each other in the making of decisions but the final power to decide rests with one party only'. Full participation, on the other hand, is defined as 'a process where each individual member of a decision-making body has equal power to determine the outcome of decisions' (Pateman, 1972, pp. 70–71). The kinds of inequities and marginalisation experienced by young people described in the first commentary of this book suggest that political participation is partial at best.

Part of the challenge created by this rhetoric of digital participation – be it from government or from those uncritically inclined to technological hype – is that it creates the false feeling of participation; that is, that participation is possible rather than building a situation in which participation actually takes place (Verba, 1961). A good example was the wave of positive media coverage about the use of Twitter during the 2009 Iranian elections and its defiance of censorship. Western media reports of a 'Twitter Revolution' overstated its actual significance, both in terms of the level of adoption by Iranians and the impact on the outcome of that election. According to *Foreign Policy* magazine blogger, Evgeny Morozov (2009), Twitter was 'of great help in terms of getting information out of [Iran]. Whether it has helped to organise protests – something that most of the media are claiming at the moment – is not at all certain'. In sum, it would appear that no particular technology was instrumental to the mobilisation of people by organisers to participate in protest or voting. (It is more likely that SMS text messaging played a more significant role than Twitter (Schectman, 2009).) The point is that a lot of the enthusiasm for the political possibilities of the 'Twitter Revolution' was based on false or unsubstantiated claims to authentic participation.

Enthusiasm for the political possibilities of ICTs often overshadows the lack of evidence as to the real effectiveness and impact of their use in deliberately making change. As Brett Solomon, GetUp!'s first executive director, said on reflection of his time with the organisation, 'Sometimes you can lose sight of how much influence you really have' (Marks, 2010, p. 29). The real impact of ICT-use to make change is still problematic and questionable. According to Marks, 'Outside election time, GetUp!'s achievements are harder to gauge. Many of its campaigns – calling, for instance, for a human rights act and tougher carbon reduction targets – have yet to produce tangible results' (Marks, 2010, p. 31).

So while the internet has the potential to 'reorient the fulcrum of control by promoting a more democratic and inclusive dialogue' and enable marginalised voices to be heard (Schuler, 2003, p. 70), evidence around actual change enabled by digital media remains scarce. What does emerge from this shifting and complex landscape is a dynamic of mediated and face-to-face interaction, characterised by forms of collaboration and engagement that challenge many conventional understandings of how people engage in change-making and participate more broadly, and how this plays out in relation to the institutional and market power of government and business.

Shifting loci of power and influence and the generational divide

The case study of SYN earlier in this chapter reveals some underlying tensions relating to the role of government and business: 'The policy-makers can't seem to keep up, relying on the private sector to deal with whatever major economic and social consequences digital communication throws up. The SYNners decided to figure it out for themselves' (Rennie, 2009, p. 235). The 'wide-scale participation of ordinary folk in media production and distribution' are engaged in new ideas and technologies that 'are emerging out of non-market-based activities – friendship groups and hobbies – outside of professionalised industry' (Rennie, 2009, p. 235).

Young people seek and respond to different ways of learning and interacting. The SYN case study illustrates this tension at the local institutional level of the school. In the prior incarnation of SYN, 3TD, students approached the initiative:

> ... with energy, engaging in a way that the school curriculum could not achieve. For the teachers, it provided a new kind of learning; students could express themselves on their own terms, resist conformity and understand the media from the other side, [but] by

teaching students to 'read' the media, but not to 'write' it, schools distanced students from the media.

(Rennie, 2009, pp. 237–241)

One US media educator has observed that 'The failure of schools and after-school programs to address the media as the predominant language of youth today, or to recognise the social and cultural contexts in which students live, has resulted in a profound disconnect' (Goodman, cited in Rennie 2009, p. 240). This disconnect occurs at both institutional and generational levels. Gradually, the teachers who began the 3TD initiative receded as it developed an increasingly youth-led approach. One of the teachers who originated what became SYN observes that adults 'have different ideas of youth empowerment from the youth they are claiming to empower' (Rennie, 2009, p. 239).

Previously, we have highlighted the untapped value of youth participation in school decision-making and civic life, both in terms of young people's engagement in schools and in their engagement as active citizens. Developments in ICTs have opened up opportunities for young people's engagement on the one hand, while on the other exacerbating the distance of politicians from these so-called 'digital natives' (a term that could have been coined by a political speech writer). As Thom Woodroofe observes in his viewpoint, there is much about contemporary politics that young people find 'repugnant'. Partly in response to these trends towards disengagement, state and federal governments are increasingly seeking to engage young people through online social networks, formal consultations, online discussion forums and representative non-government organisations, but with mixed results (e.g. see Chen & Walsh, 2010).

A cursory look at popular media reinforces the impression that many political representatives are out of touch with young people, and nowhere is this more evident than in their political use of ICTs. Recent efforts to connect to younger voters via media channels such as YouTube and social networking sites such as Facebook have, if anything, served to exacerbate the distance between young people and political representatives. Former Prime Minister Rudd's youth blog, entitled 'Helping young Australians build their own futures', was a painful example (Prime Minister of Australia, 2009). Shut down only two weeks after its launch, the blog included Rudd's own exemplar of youth achievement, bootmaker R. M. Williams, who started out at the age of 24. Though Williams is a worthy role model on one level, the cultural cringe that this painfully stiff nomination elicited from young people resonated with many across Australia. (Rudd's dual problem was one of medium *and* message.) This growing distance is in part also due to the sheer pace of technological change. The growth in Web 2.0 tools and networked communities is accompanied by new possibilities for political engagement, such as 'new virtual actions varying from an online petition to pinning down the enemy's server' (van Aelst & Walgrave, 2004, p. 114). Young people dominate this mediated landscape. Older generations need to catch up.

Despite this disconnect and distance, conventional institutions still have an important role to play, and to work outside them is unrealistic and potentially counter-productive. 'Schools still have an important role to play', Rennie writes, '[i]t's fair to say that [founding teachers] Paul Van Eeden and Colin Thompson have done more for media education and digital literacy than any other teachers in the country' (Rennie, 2009, pp. 242–243).

Young people using Web 2.0 tools and platforms increasingly expect to create and share information in more user-generated and collaborative ways, rather than be passive recipients of content. This suggests a potentially powerful shift in engagement and participation, the significance of which remains underdeveloped and unrecognised by conventional institutions of power. Where participation is vital for effective social democracy, these tools and applications are potentially powerful instruments to make change. At a deeper level, these tools are enabling a shift in the loci of power. We see this at its most extreme in the controversial release of sensitive military information by WikiLeaks. But the emergence of social movements such as GetUp! illustrate this shift in increasingly mainstream ways. Adrienne Vromen suggests that GetUp! may be Australia's 'most important civil society actor' (Vromen, cited in Marks 2010, p. 31). In Australia, Kathy Marks suggests, 'five years ago the idea of a political movement based on the internet's capacity to facilitate mass communication was positively revolutionary' (Marks, 2010, p. 28). In recent years, GetUp! has shifted its actions from the virtual to actual grassroots participation (Marks, 2010). It is significant that ICTs are used in a blended approach with face-to-face engagement and action to aggregate and amplify voices. GetUp! uses offline actions alongside email information campaigns and online petitions to extend awareness of specific issues and shift 'public opinion by forging links to the mainstream media ... to move beyond the converted, by branching out to the wider public ...' (Huijser & Little, 2008). One example of this was the use of online donations and viral marketing to fund a mainstream television advertising campaign in 2007 to influence government policy on climate change (GetUp, 2007). This suggests the way forward for the use of ICTs by social enterprise. But deep and persistent challenges remain.

Persistent challenges of the digital divide

Access defines the means, resources and opportunities available to citizens to participate (Cammaerts & Carpentier, 2005). There are still significant differences in access to, and use of, the internet across Australian geographic locations, cultural milieus and areas in which young people experience socio-economic disadvantage (Muir, 2004). Persistent challenges of access and inadequate digital literacy echo many of the issues of inclusion discussed in my commentary in Chapter 1 of this book.

By 2007, nine out of 10 Australian families had an internet connection, three quarters of which had access to broadband. Each day, Australians aged eight to 17 spent on average 1¼ hours online. Those less likely to access computers or the internet included young people from Indigenous or non-English speaking backgrounds, those not in the labour force, and those living in small country towns. Nine out of 10 young people aged 17 used a mobile phone, with young women more likely to use mobile phones than young men. Young people from relatively poorer areas used their mobile phones more frequently than those from the relatively wealthier areas. Many young people from non-English speaking backgrounds expressed reluctance to use a mobile phone (Muir et al., 2009, p. 68). This may be related to poorer internet access and use, with comparatively cheaper mobile phones becoming the main point of electronic access to information and communication. Internationally, many developing socio-economic societies are adopting mobile telephony over computer-based internet due to comparatively low costs. Relatively cheap access to mobile telephony has made it a more popular means to access information and communication than computer-based networks. According to the International Telecommunication Union (ITU), global teledensity when measured according to the per capita adoption of mobile phones will reach 100 per cent within the next decade, if not sooner (*The Economist*, 2009).

As Muir and colleagues observe, the internet can be a means to both include and exclude young people: the internet 'has great potential to bring like-minded people together and can be particularly beneficial for young people who have uncommon interests or are isolated or disconnected from their family or communities'. But as ICTs in general become more accessible, the small number of young people who do not use ICTs 'through choice or lack of access ... may become increasingly isolated as the importance of these technologies continues to grow' (Muir et al., 2009, p. 67).

Even as access to ICTs continuously improves, digital literacy remains a challenge of inclusion. As Rennie (2009, p. 235) observes in relation to SYN, 'The life of SYN is ... a story of digital literacy ... involving the ability to write, not just read, the forms and languages of digital media content ... Digital literacy is an ongoing and incomplete experiment'. ICTs can both open channels of communication and engagement, but also lead to exclusionary practices.

Conclusion

The 2008 US presidential election attracted international attention to the power of ICTs in campaigning – particularly in enabling alternative forms of fundraising. However, there is still much to be understood about the degree to which legitimate participation and influence enabled by ICTs has led to sustained, genuine political impact. As James Arvanitakis and Eric Sidoti observe in their viewpoint, while the role of ICTs dominates much of the literature on young people's political participation (more so in light of the 2008 Obama campaign) there is a lack of substantive research on the actual political influence exerted by young people using ICTs. Although the real impact of ICTs in bringing about political change remains to be seen, there is enormous transformative potential. And as Rennie (2009, p. 235) argues, 'Young people are planning their response to the hard questions: "Where does new media participation lead to?" "Who is it benefiting?"'

ICTs currently play an important but often overstated role in facilitating dialogue and enabling opportunities for social innovation and impact. They provide a useful set of tools to share information and communicate, but there is a risk of falsely elevating their significance in enabling active participation and generating sustained, genuine change. The absence of good evidence in this area suggests an important role for research in providing more concrete measures and indicators of real impact.

It is also important to note that from many young people's perspectives, the boundaries between face-to-face and online environments are blurred and fluid. That many do not differentiate between their online interactions and their face-to-face ones is significant. Based on experience from other domains of technological engagement, such as e-learning, the best approaches blend digital approaches with proven methods at the face-to-face level. Interestingly, those who develop online networks do not necessarily do so at the expense of 'real world' interaction. There is evidence from the US to suggest that users of social media are more active in general than those not engaged with online communities. The study conducted in 2008 found that 10 per cent of internet users used a social networking site for some sort of political or civic engagement (Smith et al., 2009). Most people who used an online social networking service such as Facebook, MySpace, or LinkedIn had more diverse social networks than those who did not use the internet. Fifteen per cent posted comments or images/video content on a website or blog about a political or social issue. Those who used blogs and social networking sites as an outlet for civic engagement were more active in face-to-face realms of political participation, compared both to other internet users and to those who did not use the internet at all. Half of those involved in political or community groups communicated with other group members online. Political donations were most likely to be made over the internet. The online political activity of the well-off and well-educated was likely to mirror their offline political activity. Nevertheless, the same study found that the internet:

> ... is not changing the socio-economic character of civic engagement in America. Just as in offline civic life, the well-to-do and well-educated are more likely than those less well off to participate in online political activities such as emailing a government official, signing an online petition or making a political contribution.
>
> (Smith et al., 2009).

As a means of enabling interaction and engagement, we need to ensure that ICTs are accessible to young people, and that they have the literacies to use them. SYN is a positive story of a social enterprise that has used ICTs to enhance communication, engagement and digital literacy for young people. It has experienced significant growth in both size and use of ICTs, suggesting a growing need in the youth sector. Over 5000 young people were members of SYN in 2006 after only three years of full-time broadcasting, many of whom were volunteers (Rennie, 2009). It has expanded its modes of delivery to radio, television and the web. Content creation is now a core feature of SYNners, who 'conduct a continuous conversation on the best way to create content' (Rennie, 2009, p. 242). Rennie suggests that '[f]or all of the talk of a new communications paradigm there are very few stories of the people who are actually making it. SYN is a very small enterprise where people go to learn about, and become part of, the media' (2009, p. 235).

As hybrids of corporate and third-sector organisations, the social enterprises and young social entrepreneurs discussed in case studies throughout this book are seeking to make social impact where government and other actors are unable or unmotivated. They are nimble, adaptable and thrive on innovation. They use different operating models and seek a range of channels to influence and make change. Young pioneers draw upon a range of resources, networks and approaches – often to expedite the delivery of a program, campaign or initiative. They can make change at a local level far more quickly than local government. The hybrid nature of social enterprises reflects a pragmatic and strategic attitude prevalent among young social entrepreneurs. Discouraged by slow government bureaucracy but not driven by profit, many young entrepreneurs draw from the third sector, government, corporate or all of these worlds in order to make change. And with the rollout of faster internet and next generation mobile telephony, ICTs are one of the next great frontiers of social innovation and enterprise. They can enable youth-led and youth-focused social enterprises to extend, enhance and improve how they make impact. The convergence of technology, passion and enterprise is opening up exciting new opportunities for young people to change Australia and the world.

References

Anderson, K. (Director). (2003). *In the realm of the hackers.* [Television program, broadcast 29 May 2003]. Australian Broadcasting Corporation.

Augar, N., Raitman, R., & Zhou, W. (2006). Wikis: Collaborative virtual environments. In J. Weiss, J. Nolan, J. Hunsinger & P. Trifonas (Eds.), *International handbook of virtual learning environments* (pp. 1251–1269). Springer International Handbooks of Education, Vol. 14. Netherlands: Springer.

Australian Centre for Philanthropy and Nonprofit Studies (ACPNS) & Social Traders (2010). *Finding Australia's Social Enterprise Sector (FASES).* Retrieved 8 September 2010 from: http://www.socialtraders.com.au/finding-australias-social-enterprise-sector-fases

Cammaerts, B., & Carpentier, N. (2005). The unbearable lightness of full participation in a global context: WSIS and civil society participation. Media@lse, *Electronic Working Paper 8.*

Castells, M. (2000). *The rise of the network society* (2nd ed.). Malden, MA: Blackwell Publishing.

Chen, P. J., & Walsh, L. (2010). E-Election 2007? Political competition online. *Australian Cultural History, 28*(1), 47–54.

Collin, P. (2008). The internet, youth participation policies, and the development of young people's political identities in Australia. *Journal of Youth Studies, 11*(5), 527–42.

Davis, I. (2005). 'Talis, Web 2.0 and all that'. [Internet Alchemy blog, 4 July 2005]. Retrieved 28 December 2006 from: http://blog.iandavis.com/2005/07/04/talis-web-2-0-and-all-that/

Denning, D. E. (2004). 'Activism, hacktivism, and cyberterrorism: The internet as a tool for influencing foreign policy'. [The Information Warfare Site]. Retrieved 27 February 2010 from: http://www.iwar.org.uk/cyberterror/resources/denning.htm

Dreyfus, S. (1997). *Underground: Tales of hacking, madness and obsession on the electronic frontier.* Kew, VIC: Mandarin.

The Economist (2009). Finishing the job, 24 September 2009. Retrieved 9 April 2010 from: http://www.economist.com/surveys/displaystory.cfm?story_id=14483856

GetUp (2007). Climate Ad at the AFL Grand Final! Retrieved 8 April 2011 from: https://www.getup.org.au/campaign/ClimateCleverer&id=128

Halavais, A. C. (2006). Weblogs and collaborative web publishing as learning spaces. In J. Weiss, J. Nolan, J. Hunsinger & P. Trifonas (Eds.), *International Handbook of Virtual Learning Environments*, (pp. 1216–35). Springer International Handbooks of Education, Vol. 14. Netherlands: Springer.

Huijser, H., & Little, J. (2008). 'GetUp! For what? Issues driven democracy in a transforming public sphere'. *Transformations, 16*. Retrieved 10 April 2010 from: http://www.transformationsjournal.org/journal/issue_16/article_06.shtml

Ma, L. (2009). Slacktivism: Can social media actually cause social change?. *The Age*, 1 October 2009. Retrieved 10 April 2010 from: http://www.theage.com.au/technology/technology-news/slacktivism-can-social-media-actually-cause-social-change-20090930-gcgk.html

Marks, K. (2010). GetUp! began with funding from 'trade unions, refugee campaigners and technology millionaires' in 'Exclamation Politics', *The Monthly, 61*, October, pp. 28–31.

Morozov, E. (2009). Iran elections: A Twitter revolution? *The Washington Post*, 17 June 2009. Retrieved 26 February 2009 from: http://www.washingtonpost.com/wp-dyn/content/discussion/2009/06/17/DI2009061702232.html

Muir, K. (2004). *Connecting communities with CTLCs: From the digital divide to social inclusion.* Sydney: The Smith Family.

Muir, K., Mullan, K., Powell, A., Flaxman, S., Thompson, D., & Griffiths, M. (2009). *State of Australia's young people: A report on the social, economic, health and family lives of young people.* Canberra: Australian Government Publishing Service.

Murphy, D. (2008). GetUp! pioneer goes global on internet politics. *The Sydney Morning Herald*, 7 July 2008. Retrieved 10 April 2010 from: http://www.smh.com.au/news/web/getup-pioneer-goes-global-on-internet-politics/2008/07/06/1215282694065.html

The New York Times. (1999). Hackers become an increasing threat. *The New York Times*, 7 July 1999. Retrieved 2 July 2004 from: www.nytimes.com/aponline/w/AP-Hacker-Threat.html

O'Reilly, T. (2005). 'What Is Web 2.0? Design patterns and business models for the next generation of software'. [O'Reilly website, 30 September 2005]. Retrieved 2 January 2007 from: http://www.oreillynet.com/pub/a/oreilly/tim/news/2005/09/30/what-is-web-20.html

Pateman, C. (1972). *Participation and democratic theory*. Cambridge: Cambridge University Press.

Perez, S. (2008). 'How to use social media for social change' [ReadWriteWeb, 22 May 2008]. Retrieved 10 April 2010 from: http://www.readwriteweb.com/archives/how_to_use_social_media_for_social_change.php

Prime Minister of Australia. (2009). 'Helping young Australians build their own futures' [PM's Blog]. Retrieved 8 April 2011 from: http://pmrudd.archive.dpmc.gov.au/PM_Connect/PMs_Blog/Youth_Blog

Rennie, E. (2009). A story of the digital generation. *Griffith Review*, 24, 235–43. Retrieved 1 October 2010 from: http://www.griffith.edu.au/griffithreview/campaign/Ed24_APO/Rennie_Ed24.pdf

Samuel, A. (2004). Hacktivism and the future of political participation (Doctoral thesis). Retrieved 10 April 2010 from: http://www.alexandrasamuel.com/dissertation/pdfs/index.html

Saunders G. (2010, April). *'Investing for' forum*. Presentation made at the Centre for Social Impact (CSI), The Academy, National Australia Bank, Docklands, Victoria.

Schectman, J. (2009). Iran's Twitter revolution? Maybe not yet. *BusinessWeek*, 17 June 2009. Retrieved 26 February 2009 from: http://www.businessweek.com/technology/content/jun2009/tc20090617_803990.htm

Schuler, D. (2003). Reports of the close relationship between democracy and the internet may be exaggerated. In H. Jenkins & D. Thorburn (Eds.), *Democracy and New Media* (pp. 69–84). Cambridge, MA: The MIT Press.

Servaes, J. (1999). *Communication for development. One world, multiple cultures*. Cresskill, NJ: Hampton Press.

Shannon, V. (2006). A 'more revolutionary' Web. *International Herald Tribune*, 24 May 2006. Retrieved 22 July 2006 from: http://www.iht.com/articles/2006/05/23/business/web.php

Smith, A., Schlozman, K., Verba, S., & Brady, H. (2009). 'The internet and civic engagement', Pew Internet & American Life Project. Retrieved 10 April 2010 from: http://pewinternet.org/Reports/2009/15--The-Internet-and-Civic-Engagement. aspx

Spivack, N. (2003). 'Defining microcontent.' [Nova Spivack's weblog, 10 December 2003]. Retrieved 2 January 2007 from: http://novaspivack.typepad.com/nova_ spivacks_weblog/2003/12/defining_microc.html

Stokes, G., Pitty, R., & Smith, (G.) (Eds.). (2008). *Global citizens: Australian activists for change.* Port Melbourne, VIC: Cambridge University Press.

Tapscott, D., & Williams, A. D. (2006). *Wikinomics.* London: Atlantic Books.

van Aelst, P. & Walgrave, S. (2004). New media, new movements? The role of the internet in shaping the 'anti-globalization' movement. In W. van de Donk, B. D. Loader, P. G. Nixon & D. Rucht (Eds.), *Cyberprotest: New media, citizens and social movement.* New York: Routledge.

van de Donk, W., Loader, B. D., Nixon, P. G. & Rucht, D. (Eds.). (2004). Cyberprotest: New media, citizens and social movements. New York: Routledge.

Verba, S. (1961). *Small groups and political behavior.* Princeton: Princeton University Press.

Vromen, A. (2008). Political change and the internet in Australia: introducing GetUp. In T. Hayhtio & J. Rinne (Eds.), *Citizen initiated internet politics.* Finland: Tampere University Press.

W3C. (2007). W3C semantic web activity. Retrieved 12 March 2007 from: http://www. w3.org/2001/sw/

Wikipedia. (2010). Hacktivism. Retrieved 10 April 2010 from: http://en.wikipedia.org/ wiki/Hacktivism

Conclusion

Throughout this book, we and our colleagues have presented a number of challenges that strike at the very core of what it means to be a young member of Australian society. These challenges relate to young people's experience of schooling, work, political participation and general feelings of belonging. They even call into question what it means to be young. Young people can become active citizens and agents of change provided certain conditions are in place. A cultural shift is taking place at grassroots and policy levels that suggests a more positive environment for young people as social actors and agents, but more needs to be done to address key issues that continue to inhibit and restrain their capacity to enjoy a greater role in shaping their world.

We would like to conclude this discussion by signposting some of these issues and what is required to address them.

As a starting point, we reflect on what is meant by active citizenship, and how this can function as a conceptual and practical basis for a vision of how young people can make change. We also reflect on the key problems of inequity and exclusion that marginalise and inhibit the capacity for young people to shape matters of concern to them. Many of these barriers are structural and institutionalised in central social spaces such as the school. The school is a key site through which exclusion takes place, but it also offers possibilities for positive change through innovative curriculum, pedagogy and genuine opportunities for participation in decision-making.

Beyond the classroom, there is broader change taking place that presents positive possibilities for young people seeking to influence their world. This includes the development of cross-sectoral partnerships and collaborative approaches supported by policy that recognise that it really does take a village to raise a child. It is within this space that social enterprises have emerged to address the needs of youth. But more needs to be done beyond the current policy frame to recognise these partnerships as well as the value of young people's participation within them. Greater recognition of rights is proposed to better define and protect the freedoms, entitlements and obligations of young people as active citizens.

In turn, a clearer articulation of citizenship requires a more consistent definition of what is meant by 'maturity' and 'adulthood' across personal, political, economic, civic and cultural domains. For example, we have found that young people are sent mixed messages about their maturity even though they are eligible to pay taxes. It is also necessary to challenge the myths and stereotypes that so persistently surround young people.

The need to address these issues has become all the more pressing given the profound challenges ahead, such as environmental and demographic change. It is in light of these issues – which have been raised throughout this book – that the real question emerges of 'how can we enable young people to make change?'

1   Inclusion and inequity

A recurring touchstone of this book has been the second goal of the *Melbourne Declaration on Educational Goals for Young Australians*, which affirms the importance of all young people being both 'confident and creative individuals' and 'active and informed citizens' (MCEETYA, 2008, p. 8). While this is a very worthy policy goal, we need a clearer and more common vision of what is meant by this, what needs to be in place to effectively resource its realisation, how we will know when it is (and is not) being realised, and which young people are most consistently missing out on its realisation.

The ways and degrees to which young people participate in decision- and change-making is a litmus test for the quality of Australian democracy – not only in terms of the values and institutions that underpin it, but also in the ways that it enables young people to engage beyond conventional institutions and practices, such as schools and voting, to act and innovate in practical ways. Active participation across all domains of life is essential to the fabric of democracy. John Ralston Saul (1999) once said that '[d]emocracy isn't about abstract false clear choices … it's about constantly choosing, finding, developing practical options within the common good.' Democracy, as Saul suggests, is about '[c]onstantly searching for how to express in a practical way the common good'. This is where youth-led initiatives such as Left Right Think-Tank and SYN play such a crucial role in shaping, discussing, disseminating and implementing change. They provide platforms through which young people can articulate their views and deliberate on what needs to be done to improve their worlds. Such platforms are, therefore, as central to the enactment of citizenship as any formal political practice.

This is not to suggest that citizenship is a uniform entity or experience. In fact, the experience of citizenship both binds and divides young people. For young people to become active citizens, they need to feel a sense of belonging and inclusion. The discussion and analysis in the first part of this book looked at different dimensions of this inclusion by outlining some of the ways that many young people feel marginalised: through racism; through exclusion from political participation; and through exclusion from the worlds of work and post-school education and the social and economic benefits that they offer.

Australian public policy makes it clear that all young people should have an active role in the development of the nation as a whole and in their own lives. It is clear that this ambition will not be realised without deep thinking about, and genuine responses to, the fundamental forms of inequity and exclusion that manifest across the political, educational, cultural, social and economic dimensions of young people's lives.

We know, for example, that young people from Indigenous and migrant backgrounds experience racism more intensely than other groups, but the evidence suggests that the experience of racism is pervasive in many young people's lives. The risk of cultural exclusion is not tied to any single ethnic group, although some are clearly more vulnerable than others.

From an economic and educational perspective, we know that young people are increasingly segregated by a growing divide in educational achievement and family economic and cultural assets, with the most economically vulnerable populations of young people also the most likely to fail according to current educational measures and standards. These young people live in regional and remote areas, come from disadvantaged backgrounds and leave school before Year 11 or 12. Further to this, our education systems privilege certain cultural and social traditions and measures of success, especially the pathway to higher education. As Johanna Wyn argues, this works against the interests of those young people 'whose cultural and social experience diverge from traditional school cultures'.

New approaches are overdue that will shift these longstanding patterns of unequal outcomes and systemic socio-economic barriers to participation. New thinking is needed about how we can better open up new pathways to earning and learning, and, more broadly, how we can provide opportunities for active citizenship to flourish across all domains of life for all young people.

From a government perspective, there is also a need to rethink and more carefully articulate what is meant by social inclusion. This has become the touchstone for much educational and youth policy, but its real meanings and implications remain unclear. Recent Australian governments have adopted a hollow policy narrative of social cohesion and inclusion; this narrative privileges a minimal definition of citizenship loaded with particularly narrow historical and economic notions of identity that do not connect with the richly diverse, lived experiences of young people in Australia. An example comes from the major pillar of the former Rudd government's policy narrative of social inclusion, which sought to shape the capacity of young people to 'Earn or Learn'. This agenda has attempted to promote smoother transitions from school to work, post-school study and training as part of a broader agenda of social inclusion with a focus on economic wellbeing and 'working families'. But the challenges for young people are more complex than this kind of policy narrative allows. They are influenced by a much broader range of factors that include their cultural heritage and background, access to technology and geographic location, as well as wider forces such as demographic change and long-term labour-market trends. When thinking about what social inclusion means in Australia, it is important that we address these challenges with the rich diversity of young people and the complexity of their experience in mind. Beyond the scope of this book, this includes the needs of those with disabilities, those experiencing problems with mental health and those experiencing isolation, among others.

2   The school as a site for institutional reform

Many of our public institutions both reflect and reinforce these structural and systemic barriers to belonging, connection and participation. As we have seen throughout this book, schools in particular are ideal institutions for the nurturing of active citizenship, but their capacity to do so is constricted by longstanding cultural, institutional and practical barriers. Overcoming these requires serious long-term attention to socio-economic disadvantage and to the development of innovative curriculum, pedagogy and targeted programs such as civics and citizenship education to better foster inclusion, participation and young people's sense of agency.

What we mean by innovative curriculum is that which engages young people by drawing on their own experience, enables them to make connections between their current life circumstances and wider social and economic processes, and that involves them in decision-making in the classroom, the school and the community through negotiated learning processes. Reflecting on the development of the new Australian curriculum, Allan Luke (2010, p. 59) has suggested that 'any official curriculum … comes to ground via an enacted curriculum of teaching and learning events "lived" by students and teachers'. He argues for 'visible connections of school knowledge to everyday civic, cultural, political and social life' (Luke, 2010, p. 61). This approach has the wider benefit of developing young people's civic dispositions. Through these visible connections, young people can better understand what needs to be done to make change and how they are connected to it.

To date, the capacity of young people to make change has been constrained by a limited educational vision and a limited language of democratic possibility. There remains an emptiness at the heart of Australian citizenship that emphasises it as a legal status only and which gives primacy to a narrow form of economic participation that is far from the vision outlined by the Ministerial Council in the *Melbourne Declaration*.

As Kymlicka and Norman (1994, p. 352) write, 'the health and stability of a modern democracy depends, not only on the justice of its "basic structure" but also on the qualities and attitudes of its citizens'. Curriculum therefore needs to be recast to reflect a more dynamic conception of citizenship. It could draw from the collaborative and user-generated benefits of Web 2.0 technological platforms and tools to create genuine spaces for young people's participation and the development of their leadership, available in the places where they live and in forms that are relevant to them. Many state governments have already developed a sound basis from which to do this, but more can be done across classrooms and other learning environments by drawing from the wealth of international best practice. Fostering participation and engagement is paramount.

In Chapter 2, Johanna Wyn has outlined some of the core principles and examples of good educational practice in youth participation. Student Action Teams in Victorian primary and secondary schools, for example, place high value on the capacity of students to make a contribution to their learning in school. Using participatory approaches, teachers can design pedagogies to suit the circumstances of young people who are disengaged from school. With the erosion of boundaries between study and work, and childhood and adulthood, student participation is valuable as a means of incorporating the perspectives and experiences of these young people into the classroom.

Where schools do foster youth participation, how do we know that they are doing this well? Through measures of educational assessment, we as a society send a distinct message about our expectations of young people, what success means at school and the kind of society in which we want to live. It sends a message to young people as to whether or not they can make change as active and valuable agents who can meaningfully contribute to shaping society. Current measures of assessment such as the National Assessment Program – Literacy and Numeracy (NAPLAN) reflect an over-reliance on limited educational indicators of engagement, success and participation. The current goals of schooling come to young people from 'on high' from bodies such as the Ministerial Council on Education, Employment, Training and Youth Affairs (now the Ministerial Council on Education, Early Childhood Development and Youth Affairs), which is responsible for the *Melbourne Declaration*. How can we connect these goals more closely with the rich and real lives of young people?

Johanna points out that despite its emphasis on the importance of young people as involved citizens responsible for their education, recent education policy initiatives such as the development of an Australian Curriculum have been delimited by their lack of involvement of young people. Another example is the Australian government's Compact with Young Australians, which features a National Youth Participation Requirement that rightly emphasises the importance of full participation in schooling (or an approved equivalent) to Year 10, then at least 25 hours per week participation in education, training or employment, or a combination of these activities until age 17 (Department of Education, Employment & Workplace Relations, 2009). Bundled with this requirement, however, are changes to the Youth Allowance. While seeking to benefit young people in regional and remote communities, the punitive undertone of this requirement reflects a policy narrative largely defined by an economic world view and underpinned by a narrow definition of success in life as 'learning and earning'. Following Johanna's discussion, common goals for educational success are needed that are developed and held by young people as well as by educators and parents.

To expand our notion of civic engagement and citizenship, we need better measurements of youth participation itself that draw on broader and more sophisticated notions of social capital and wellbeing. What does the case study from Melbourne Girls' College show if not the capacity of young people to act in ways that build social capital? This is challenging, as much of the social value of participation is difficult to measure, especially within the conventional tools that we currently have at our disposal. At the very least, we need a set of standards, an underpinning set of principles, and a vision of active citizenship that moves beyond its current contested or unarticulated definitions. The challenges to developing these are many. They include teachers who are time-poor and an environment increasingly driven by very limited notions of educational success. There is the risk that in an environment that is overly concerned with measurement, educational participation may become just another task that is linked to narrow notions of success or failure and that all students are expected to undertake. As Muir and her colleagues (2009) suggest, a disposition to engage is unlikely to develop by forcing young people to participate. In fact, compelling young people to engage in civic activities can have a deterring effect. It is in the very nature of participation that it is an agentic and self-motivated activity and orientation to the world: it is not something that can be mandated and measured through an imposed curriculum and assessment.

We have already seen the failure of civics and citizenship education to capture the imagination of young people. Traditionally, civics education has been concerned with the instruction, study and learning of citizenship and its associated rights and duties. Its curriculum has focused on providing information about the historical development of national identity, civic life, politics and government. How effective civics and citizenship education works in practice is contested and open to interpretation, however. Mellor (2003) rightly asserts that '[w]ithout civic knowledge and a disposition to engage, a person cannot effectively practise citizenship'. Kat Ettwell from OUTthere, who appears in our case study in Chapter 1, acknowledges a need to 'learn more about how the Australian government works ... how you can get things passed with the government; how you get people to listen to you'. Her strategic interest in linking knowledge of how government works to her own social enterprise provides insight into how we can start to rethink the teaching of civics and citizenship in schools.

The key to effective citizenship education is that students have opportunities to experience, practise and develop civic competencies. But opportunities for young people to experience and develop these in practice are constrained by three factors.

Firstly, the institutional structures of schooling have traditionally discouraged student participation in decision-making. Ironically, despite the good intentions of its creators, civics and citizenship education has contributed to sending a mixed message to young people about democratic citizenship. It has tended to be inhibited by a sterile view of democracy disconnected from the experiences of young people, and has overlooked or underplayed their involvement as active agents as well as the educative value of their participation in collective decision-making. Murray Print (1996) has long argued that citizenship education needs to be 'based on positive views of student learning through participation', yet within the hierarchical, didactic environments of most classrooms, young people learn that democracy is important but do not experience it in practice.

Secondly, civics and citizenship education has been relegated to the periphery of the core curriculum as an add-on. This sits oddly with the apparent policy enthusiasm for the use of the curriculum to engage young people as active citizens. Thirdly, and further to this, there needs to be a far better articulation of what active citizenship actually looks like, and its means and modes of expression across different domains and stages of life. It cannot be something that exists as a purely abstract notion or that only begins once one reaches voting age.

A participatory approach to citizenship encourages the acquisition of knowledge and skills through active participation in formal institutional settings such as schools and across informal contexts (e.g. through voluntary engagement in community organisations, membership of web-based social movements, or through the exercise of market power through consumer choice). Young people need to be able to connect the experience of participation to other parts of their lives: in work, at home and across digital networks. This is unlikely to happen unless we first build the capacity of schools to recognise and support young people's participation.

3   Structural change beyond the classroom

Schools are not the only key social institutions whose operations need to be reassessed. What does it mean for key social and political structures that young people are routinely bypassing them? Conventional political pathways are not working for many young people. They are not reflective of the realities of contemporary life. An ancillary question to Mellor's observations described above is whether the conditions are available for civic dispositions to develop that are not just oriented towards formal, conventional pathways such as voting or membership of a political party or trade union.

The evidence certainly suggests that young people may define themselves as 'active and informed' in different and new ways to what is implied in the *Declaration*. As research by the Whitlam Institute has found, young people participate in activities that 'deliver short-term, visible and efficacious outcomes that eschew traditional hierarchies, operate through transparent processes and afford agency' (Arvanitakis & Marren, 2009, p. 6). As the case studies have shown, these activities are frequently taking place through new vehicles such as social enterprises or using new media to create social movements at local and national levels. GetUp! is one strong example of this. Young people often reject conventional political institutions that are seen to inhibit their capacity to voice concerns about their needs and to drive social change. Of particular significance is that many young people who are seeking to bring about change do not necessarily categorise their activity as being 'political'. This trend escapes much of the current discourse and policy narrative concerning youth.

The case study of Jack Hegarty, for example, presents a snapshot of a vibrant, articulate young person who is driven to make social change but is sometimes discouraged by the conventional pathways available through local government. His feelings of alienation are consistent with the findings cited by James Arvanitakis and Eric Sidoti in their viewpoint: 'young people are politically engaged while Politically ambivalent'. The dynamic between young people's negative attitudes to formal Politics versus their engagement in informal political activities suggests that some young people are disconnected from conventional political participation, while others cannot see or understand how they might choose to participate instead.

As Celia Hannon and Charlie Tims have pointed out in relation to the British context, 'young people are not simply the passive subjects of social and political change' (2010, p. 19). Instead, they are actively shaping society and challenging us to rethink how we articulate their belonging and membership through citizenship and social action. At the same time, as Hannon and Tims warn, too many young people are being excluded from these emerging opportunities for participation.

Other positive developments suggest new possibilities for young people to bring about change.

We have found that the conventional lens through which we understand 'the political' does not enable us to see many of the ways that young people are seeking to make change. The young social entrepreneurs described by Cheryl Kernot and Thom Woodroofe are exploring alternative means of change-making. They have a strong disposition to engage, but not through conventional pathways. The use of ICTs to extend the reach and impact of youth-led social enterprises are also enabling young people to open up new spaces, tools and opportunities for participation.

Underpinning the capacity for young people to shape their world is a changing landscape in which government is working differently with business and non-government organisations. Though still very much in a developmental phase at the time of writing, this glacial shift in attitude offers new opportunities for young people to lead change through third-sector organisations, such as those advocating for youth, or through social enterprises with youth-oriented agendas.

Echoing the Third Way politics of the United Kingdom, recent Australian governments at state and federal levels have begun to develop policy and mechanisms to enable non-government bodies to play a greater and more direct role in social change through partnership and collaboration in areas of public policy and community development.

National Compact: Working Together reflects a move by government to recognise and consolidate relations with third-sector organisations (Commonwealth of Australia, 2010). This includes a more active role for business to work with government and non-government organisations beyond conventional strategies of corporate social responsibility. Many companies now explicitly seek greater involvement in a range of social policy domains by sharing their resources and expertise in more targeted and long-term ways. Education policy has made great strides in explicitly recognising the importance of the development of business and philanthropic partnerships with schools and other educational institutions and providers.

These broader shifts towards collaboration and dialogue evident in business and policy approaches to social change suggest an environment increasingly favourable to social enterprise as a means for addressing the social, economic and political challenges of the 21st century. As suggested above, Web 2.0 tools and applications offer a range of tools that are ideally suited to this environment. But some of the greatest challenges lie ahead in translating this dialogue to action.

While this growing recognition by governments and business of the importance of cross-sectoral partnerships is welcome, more needs to be done to articulate their relevance to youth policy. There needs to be a stronger recognition of the importance of cross-sectoral partnerships in enabling young people and the youth sector to influence and shape their communities and society.

4 Maturity and participation: Mixed messages, myths and contradictions

Throughout this book, a recurrent theme has been the mixed messages sent to young people about their capacity to influence and make change. The ways by which schools rhetorically promote ideas of democracy while actually discouraging participation is one example of the way that current institutions and structures send and reinforce conflicting messages about young people and how their participation is formally recognised. The juxtaposition of the legal recognition of what constitutes maturity to be taxed versus the entitlement to vote is another. These messages reinforce contradictory notions of maturity, responsibility and 'the coming of age', and reflect a deeper schism between how pathways to adulthood are recognised differently across economic, educational, cultural and legal spheres of life.

Young people are clearly frustrated that they are not being heard or taken seriously. The case studies of Young Social Pioneers and the Whitlam Institute's research into young people imagining a new democracy confirm this frustration. As James Arvanitakis and Eric Sidoti found, the extent of young people's engagement within informal politics 'is disguised to some extent because it adopts forms that are often not understood, and frequently dismissed'. Returning to the astute observation of one young person cited earlier in this book: 'young people are already active – just in ways not always understood' (Arvanitakis & Marren, 2009, p. 6). We need to understand better the emergent ways and spaces where young people are exerting real power. This ideally begins by really listening to young people. Government efforts to engage young people in dialogue or through consultation have had very limited success. Sometimes, in fact, they have had the opposite effect. When Shona Cools was invited to join the Youth 2020 summit, she found it to be 'a fairly tokenistic process' whereby the 'parameters of what we were able to address were actually deliberately set'. Her experience will be familiar to many young people. In 2009, the then Minister for Early Childhood Education, Child Care and Youth, Kate Ellis, notoriously failed to show up to launch the State of Australia's Young People report and gather ideas for the National Strategy for Young Australians. A 22-year-old who had flown to Canberra to meet Minister Ellis described the turn of events as uninspiring and disappointing (Crikey, 2009).

A major challenge for government is to genuinely listen and talk to young people. The rhetoric or illusion of participation is more dangerous than the absence of it. It promotes disaffection and cynicism. Tokenistic efforts to engage young people that don't actively take their considerations into decision-making ensure civic disengagement and disenchantment.

There is also a darker underbelly to the rhetoric of participation that seeks to blame young people for their circumstances or to construct them as 'the problem' without acknowledging the deeper structural and institutional factors that may be contributing to those circumstances. The Rudd government's 'Earn or Learn' strategy, for example, followed a longer-term trajectory of policy thinking according to which the locus of change was placed upon young people, rather than on the deeper challenges of unemployment and a shifting labour market. Bessant (2009) argues that 'too many times in the past three decades, governments are treating the unemployed, in this case young people, as the problem – rather than addressing the real need, which is for more jobs'. She suggests that governments have evaded the broader structural problems of unemployment, while inflaming public anxiety about 'unemployed youth'. The popular media frequently depicts 'Gen Y' as a group of young people characterised by greater fluidity in their career pathways, seeking more choice and changing jobs more frequently in their career than their parents. For many, this may be less a function of choice than of necessity.

The evidence is that this generation seeks many of the same basic qualities of life as any other generation. The Longitudinal Surveys of Australian Youth, for example, provide insight into young people's attitudes to earning and learning in relation to broader measures of wellbeing (see http://www.lsay.edu.au/index.html). In 2007, young adults in full-time work were much more likely to be very happy about their career prospects, their future, their life as a whole, and their standard of living, in comparison to part-time workers, those who were unemployed or not in the labour force (Robinson & Lamb, 2009). Young people such as apprentices who have money in their pocket and a sense of a career pathway are happier about their life in general (Dockery, 2010). The evidence also suggests that part-time work, unemployment or withdrawal from the labour force may have a negative impact on young people's levels of satisfaction with non-economic aspects of their lives, such as their use of spare time, social life and independence (Hillman & McMillan, 2005). The bottom line, then, is that most young people seek security just like anyone else. But beyond this, they are highly differentiated from other demographic groups, with different needs, aspirations and views of the world. Striking the right balance between this diversity and what is common to all becomes possible only once we have addressed the cultural and structural conditions needed to give a voice to young people and empower them to speak out, to articulate their needs and, where necessary, to make change.

At the same time, we need to constantly question this notion of empowerment. Even the most passionate advocates need to critically interrogate and explode the myths and plaster idols of the young leader as 'hero'. To either valorise or enshrine participation as a requisite of young people is to institutionalise it in ways that may be unhelpful. As we have already said, such institutionalisation risks reducing participation to an exercise in either compliance or compulsion. It risks imposing adult-centric or controlled forms of participation upon young people that rob them of the very agency that most motivates them to act. It also risks the systematic overlooking of those young people who may not wish to lead, or may not wish to lead in ways that are highly visible, but who still require their views and needs to be heard and counted. We may not be able to mandate participation, therefore, but we must make every opportunity for it to take place, in spheres and in ways determined by young people themselves.

5   The roads ahead

Young people can make change, but they can't do it alone. They need a supportive environment that includes the right resources and partnerships. The imperative to enable the conditions and dispositions of active citizenship becomes all the more important in light of the challenges faced by young people living in the 21st century.

Rejecting the media focus and adversarial nature of conventional party politics as 'increasingly repugnant', Thom Woodroofe describes 'a generation confronted by some of the greatest challenges to the environment, to the economy and to so many other parts of their society in which their children would be born'. Thom notes how his own perception of what constituted involvement in his community grew in scope and sophistication over time; his experience reflects the awareness of many young people of the global playing field in which their ideas and actions can have impact. It also reflects the real need for this impact given the clear failure of existing discourses and approaches to emerging global problems, such as environmental degradation. Environmental degradation and resource scarcity, in particular, are perhaps the two greatest challenges facing young people. Climate change is already affecting human mobility by forcing the migration of some groups while restricting the movement of others. Described as 'the first climate refugees', inhabitants of The Carteret Islands, for example, have been forced to evacuate their Pacific homes (Morton, 2009) as a result of climate change.

The prioritisation of economic world views over other dimensions of life has resulted in hollow and ineffective policy discourses of inclusion and reform. This is not to diminish the significance of economic concerns in contemporary life, but the domination of market-based solutions is in itself an exclusionary discourse. As Johanna observes in her personal perspective of student participation: '[r]elying on market forces to bring about educational change through patterns of educational consumption by discerning parents is a woefully inadequate way to create improved educational outcomes – education is too important to be left to market forces'. This is equally applicable to how we think about the development of young people as active citizens. Data from the World Values Survey, in which the views of young Australians on aspects of citizenship are compared with those of young people in other countries, suggest many similarities in world views. While young adults in Australia see economic growth as important, the majority indicate that protecting the environment should have even greater priority, echoing other research and evidence to emerge during the last few years (Lamb, Robinson & Walstab, 2010).

Demographic change is another – and highly underestimated – challenge facing young people in the years ahead. Young people aged 12 to 24 currently represent around one-fifth of the Australian population. Around two in three 12- to 19-year-olds live at home with two parents, with a further 20 per cent living with one parent. Young people are also residing for longer periods of time with their parents (Muir et al., 2009). As young people undertake more study and training further into life, this defers their entry into the paths that form the basis of long-term material wellbeing, financial security and contribution to the broader economy. Coupled with this trend towards later economic participation is the challenge of Australia's ageing population. As a result of sustained low levels of fertility combined with an increasing life expectancy at birth, the age composition of Australia's population is expected to change considerably over the next 50 years. It is expected that by the middle of this century there will be a greater proportion of people aged 65 years and over, and a lower proportion of people aged under 15 years. ABS statistics indicate that where young people under the age of 15 years made up just under 20 per cent of the total population in 2007, this proportion is expected to decrease to between 15 to 18 per cent by 2056. In contrast to this, the proportion of the population aged 65 years and over is expected to grow from 13 per cent to between 23 and 55 per cent during the same period. The proportion of Australians over 85 years old could increase from 1.6 per cent to up to 7.3 per cent during this time-frame (Australian Bureau of Statistics, 2008).

This ageing population may have a profound impact upon young people seeking employment, particularly as we see movement towards increasing the age of retirement and a growing corporate interest in re-employing people from older demographic groups. Aside from the implications of caring for an ageing population, the delaying of retirement to later in life will increasingly impact upon young people's opportunities to get full-time work in an increasingly competitive and saturated labour market. This demographic shift also has broader social implications that will affect young people in the future.

One looming challenge related to this demographic trend is the growing perception of inter-generational inequality. Factors such as declining opportunities for full-time employment, growing costs of education and the difficulty for many young people in entering the housing market all suggest the possibility of intergenerational inequalities of opportunity and access, a trend already evident in the United Kingdom (Hannon & Tims, 2010). In countries more deeply affected by the global financial crisis, such as England, a question now asked for the first time is: 'will our children inherit a quality of life worse than their parents?' This trend also suggests the possibility of growing resentment by young people towards older generations, who are the main beneficiaries of decades of economic growth.

These environmental, economic and demographic trends towards greater scarcity reinforce the need to understand and address the interdependency and shared needs of all people. The need to underpin all human development with a shared belief in the common good is no longer either an aspiration or an abstraction: it is now a necessity.

With the need to identify this shared belief comes an imperative to develop better ways of engaging young people and improving how we recognise their contributions to Australia's cultural, social, political and economic development. This is where the formal recognition of a Bill of Rights for all Australians could play a critical role. The articulation of such a Bill would not only serve as a platform to articulate principles of freedom, entitlement and obligation, but could also be developed in such a way that young people could own and value it as a shared symbolic and legal basis for active citizenship. A robust public debate, properly developed, could serve as a means of engaging young people in a reflection about what is common to all in contemporary Australian life (and to people universally) as a basis for shaping a vision of active citizenship.

Articulating what active citizenship looks like in practice has been proposed as one part of this process. Incorporating this understanding into how we measure and promote educational success, and success in life in general, is another. We need to understand better the ways in which young people are participating in making change that are not recognised within current frameworks. We also need to understand better the implications of technology in these activities – when it has led to genuine impact and when it hasn't. All of these actions require us to first move beyond the rhetoric, the stereotyping and the mixed messages that surround young people and their capacity to shape their world.

If young people have become society's drivers for change, as Cheryl Kernot suggests in the Foreword, then we have an obligation to ensure that the conditions, resources and opportunities are available for them to do so. This includes the support of agencies, individuals and governments across sectors and jurisdictions. As important, we need to nurture and provide opportunities for young people to lead change and play a meaningful role in shaping their world. Ultimately, it is their confidence, ideas, passion, experience and voice that will make a difference.

It really is in their own hands.

References

Arvanitakis, J., & Marren, S. (2009). *Putting the politics back into Politics: Young people and democracy in Australia*. (Discussion paper). Sydney: Whitlam Institute.

Australian Bureau of Statistics (2008). Population Projections, Australia, 2006 to 2101. Retrieved 28 June 2010 from: http://www.abs.gov.au/ausstats/abs@.nsf/mf/3222.0

Bessant, J. (2009). 'Jobless young need opportunities not punishment'. *The Age*, 8 May 2009. Retrieved 6 August 2010 from: http://www.theage.com.au/opinion/jobless-young-need-opportunities-not-punishment-20090507-awk5.html

Commonwealth of Australia. (2010). *National compact: Working together*. Retrieved 2 April 2010 from: http://www.nationalcompact.gov.au/wordpress/wp-content/uploads/Nat_compact.pdf

Crikey (2009). 'Kate Ellis and the youth roundtable that wasn't.' [Crikey website, 23 October 2009]. Retrieved 29 October 2009 from: http://www.crikey.com.au/2009/10/23/kate-ellis-and-the-youth-roundtable-that-wasnt/

Department of Education, Employment & Workplace Relations (DEEWR). (2009). *Compact with young Australians.* Accessed 2 April 2010 at: http://www.deewr.gov.au/Youth/YouthAttainmentandTransitions/Pages/compact.aspx

Dockery, A. M. (2010). *Education and happiness in the school-to-work transition.* South Australia: The National Centre for Vocational Educational Research (NCVER).

Hannon, C., & Tims, C. (2010). *An anatomy of youth.* London: Demos.

Hillman, K., & McMillan, J. (2005). *Life satisfaction of young Australians: Relationships between further education, training and employment and general and career satisfaction.* Melbourne: Australian Council for Educational Research.

Kymlicka, W., & Norman, W. (1994). Return of the citizen: A survey of recent work on citizenship theory. *Ethics, 104*(2), 352–81.

Lamb, S., Robinson, L., & Walstab, A. (2010). *How Young People are Faring 2010.* Melbourne: The Foundation for Young Australians.

Luke, A. (2010). Will the Australian national curriculum up the intellectual ante in classrooms? *Curriculum Perspectives, 30*(3), 59–54.

Mellor, S. (2003). 'Solving some civics and citizenship education conundrums'. *Civics and citizenship education.* [Curriculum Corporation website]. Retrieved 20 February 2010 from: http://www.curriculum.edu.au/cce/default.asp?id=9318

Ministerial Council on Education, Employment, Training and Youth Affairs (MCEETYA). (2008). *Melbourne Declaration on Educational Goals for Young Australians.* Retrieved 2 April 2010 from: http:// www.mceetya.edu.au/mceecdya/default.asp?id=25979

Morton, A. (2009). First climate refugees start move to new island home. *The Age,* 29 July 2009. Retrieved 2 April 2010 from: http://www.theage.com.au/national/first-climate-refugees-start-move-to-new-island-home-20090728-e06x.html

Muir, K., Mullan, K., Powell, A., Flaxman, S., Thompson, D., & Griffiths, M. (2009). *State of Australia's young people: A report on the social, economic, health and family lives of young people.* NSW: Social Policy Research Centre, University of New South Wales.

Print, M. (1996). Pedagogical strategies for civics and citizenship education (Commissioned paper). Melbourne: Curriculum Corporation.

Robinson, L., & Lamb, S. (2009). *How Young People are Faring 2009.* Melbourne: The Foundation for Young Australians.

Saul, J. R. (1999). *Democracy and globalisation.* Lecture organised by Social Change Media, University of New South Wales, Sydney. Retrieved 2 April 2010 from: http://www.abc.net.au/specials/saul/fulltext.htm

Index